LOU REED *In His Own Words*

Nick Johnstone

Lou Reed
"Talking"

OMNIBUS PRESS

LOU REED *Talking*

CONTENTS

 **CONTENTS**

"Lou Reed is to New York what Mark Twain is to Dublin." **BONO 2004**

"Lou Reed is a completely depraved pervert and pathetic death dwarf and everything else you want to think he is. Lou Reed is the guy that gave dignity and poetry and rock 'n' roll to smack, speed, homosexuality, sadomasochism, murder, misogyny, stumblebum passivity and suicide." LESTER BANGS 1975

Over a forty year career, Lou Reed has rhythmically burned brightly and burned out. Writing always about himself as a microcosm of his beloved New York City, Reed is the consummate New York artist. A rigidly expert guitar player, in the rough hewn, stripped down, three chord brilliant manner of Keith Richards, he has alternately confounded and delighted critics and fans, his eclectic body of work to date a bombastic, erratic zig-zag across the face of rock 'n' roll. Today, he's in his sixties and still going strong, a survivor who has proudly lived the rock 'n' roll lifestyle to the hilt and lived to tell the tale, documenting along the way each skid off the road with relish, precision, a thumping rock beat and that instantly recognisable Lou Reed talk-sing voice.

Introduction

The Lou Reed story starts on March 2, 1942 when he was born Lewis Alan Reed to a Jewish New York family at Beth El Hospital in Brooklyn. His father, Sidney George Reed, was a tax accountant. His mother Toby Futterman Reed, a one-time beauty queen turned housewife and doting mother. When Lewis was five, the Reeds had a second child, a daughter this time, who they named Elizabeth. In 1953, the family moved from their apartment in Brooklyn to a house in Freeport, Long Island. After graduating from Carolyn G. Atkinson Elementary, Lewis started at Freeport High School in 1956. "I started out in the Brooklyn Public School System and have hated all forms of school and authority ever since," he later said of those years. Infatuated with the emerging rock 'n' roll sounds on the radio,

Lewis took to calling himself Lou, learned to play guitar, started writing songs and formed a band in 1954. He released his first single, 'So Blue', a year later.

Concurrent to discovering rock 'n' roll as an outlet from the stifling restrictions of suburbia, Lou also found himself passing through emotional turbulence above and beyond the usual clichéd adolescent turmoil. He raged explosively against his parents, rejecting their values. Prone to wild mood swings that rocked the Reed household, he also found himself increasingly attracted to the same sex. In response, his parents sent him for psychiatric evaluation at the Creedmore State Psychiatric Hospital. A treatment plan – electro shock treatment three times a week for eight weeks - was designed to 'cure' Lou of his erratic moods and homosexual desires. The effects were devastating, as he later explained: "You can't read a book because you get to page seventeen and you have to go right back to page one again. Or if you put the book down for an hour and went back to pick up where you started, you didn't remember the pages you read. You had to start all over. If you walked around the block, you forgot where you were." His fury at his parents for sanctioning this barbaric treatment was eventually given vent through the song 'Kill Your Sons', a key track on the 1974 album *Sally Can't Dance*.

In Autumn 1959, Lou enrolled at NYU, the campus close to Payne Whitney psychiatric clinic, where he was still undergoing shock treatments, being treated with tranquilisers and meeting with a psychiatrist three times a week. By spring 1960, Lou had dropped out of NYU and transferred to Syracuse University in Upstate New York, where he immersed himself in philosophy: "I was very into

Hegel, Sartre, Kierkergaard. After you finish reading
Kierkergaard, you feel like something horrible has happened
to you – fear and nothing. That's where I was coming from."
He also discovered Beat writers like Allen Ginsberg, Jack Kerouac
and William Burroughs, all of whose writing struck a chord. Music
was still his everything though. Lou managed to hustle his way into
getting his own show on the college radio station, where the playlist
promoted his eclectic tastes: "I was a very big fan of Ornette
Coleman, Cecil Taylor, Archie Shepp. Then James Brown, the doo-wop
groups, and rockabilly."

Resolutely a loner and outsider, Lou devoted his time to exploring
black music and tentatively dating girls. His first serious girlfriend
was Shelley Albin. Not that this put an end to his interest in the local
gay scene: "I felt very bad about it because I had a girlfriend and I
was always going out on the side." During this time, he met a fellow
campus music enthusiast – Sterling Morrison – and discovered an
appetite for drugs and thrill-seeking – three discoveries that would
define the years to come.

Once had settled at Syracuse, three further significant things happened. One, Lou formed a band called LA & The Eldorados and knew right away that playing rock 'n' roll gave him a supreme purpose. Two, he met his mentor – a drug and drink addled poet called Delmore Schwartz who had stumbled on campus to teach Creative Writing. Charismatic, doomed, tragic, Lou immediately fell under Schwartz' spell. The sozzled bard taught Lou about literature and decadent living and under his influence, Lou further experimented with drugs. According to Victor Bockris' biography, *Lou Reed*, at this time, Lou was flirting in particular with LSD and heroin. Three, he saw a concert on campus by a young verbose folksinger called Bob Dylan and stood in the crowd, mesmerised, knowing this was a pathway he was destined to follow. Then, in June 1964, as Lou graduated from Syracuse with a Bachelor of Arts in Literature, he fell violently sick with a dose of hepatitus - which he claimed to have picked up by needle-sharing. Moving back home, he successfully dodged the draft and fought off his parents' insistence that he join the family accounting business. Instead, Lou took a backroom job writing pop songs for Pickwick International, a job that lasted from September 1964 until February 1965.

During this gun-for-hire era, Lou penned and recorded a single called 'The Ostrich' for a make-believe band called The Primitives. When Pickwick received calls asking for the band to perform the song, they told Lou that they needed to assemble a makeshift band who could back him for promotional appearances. In their endeavours to create a phantom band, Lou was introduced to a student of avant-garde music, John Cale, a young Welshman decamped to New York, presently in the employ of LaMonte Young's Theater Of Eternal Music. Although 'The Ostrich' failed to materialise into a hit, thus rendering The Primitives defunct, Lou and Cale began hanging out, striking up a friendship and musical partnership. Under Cale's influence, Lou quit Pickwick and the odd couple concentrated on creating a new kind of music, one that married Lou's love of rock 'n' roll to Cale's love of all things avant garde to the gritty literary musings of the Beat writers.

Then Lou ran into Sterling Morrison in the West Village and talked the guitar player into fleshing out a band – The Warlocks – that now included Angus MacLise on drums. Right from the start of this new

INTRODUCTION

musical collaboration, Sterling was bemused by Lou's erratic moods: "I love Lou but he has what must be a fragmented personality, so you're never too sure under any conditions what you're going to have to deal with. He'll be boyishly charming, naïve – Lou is very charming when he wants to be. Or he will be vicious – and if he is, you have to figure out what's stoking the fire. What drug is he on or what mad diet? He had all sorts of strange dietary theories. He'd eat nothing, live on wheat husks. He was always trying to move mentally and spiritually to some place where no one had ever gone before."

By late 1965, they had renamed themselves The Velvet Underground and were in possession of a cluster of ground-breaking songs like 'Heroin', 'Venus In Furs', 'Black Angels Death Song' and 'Wrap Your Troubles In Dreams'. They had also lost Angus Maclise and replaced him with Mo Tucker, a girl drummer from Long Island.

The new quartet made their live debut on December 11th 1965 at the Summit High School in Summit, New Jersey. Meanwhile, across town, the pop artist Andy Warhol, was hosting a burgeoning scene of envelope-pushing art scene characters at his famous Factory. He was also looking to manage a suitably out-there band. Tipped off, in The Velvet Underground he found exactly what he was looking for. Overnight, they were swept into Warhol's entourage and handed a glamorous German female chanteuse called simply Nico. Throughout 1966, they became the house band at the Factory, Warhol's play-things, a band making a totally new sound. The buzz climaxed with their recorded debut, *The Velvet Underground And Nico*, released in 1967. With its peeling banana Warhol designed cover and seminal songs – the blueprint for so much 'alternative' music to come the record stands up today as one of the greatest rock records of all time.

Their peak had already happened though and first Nico and then Andy Warhol were ejected from the band's inner circle. By 1968's *White Light/White Heat*, inner band tensions, notably a power struggle and war of egos between Lou and Cale, had splintered the magic formula and Cale was fired from the band on Lou's orders. Drafting in Doug Yule, the band's eponymously titled third album, *The Velvet Underground*, released in 1969, was a poppier, gentler affair, moving away from the noise freakouts of *White light/White Heat*

towards a new mood of introspection and melody. By 1970 *Loaded*, the band's fourth and final studio album, Lou's muse had meandered and with Doug Yule wanting an ever more prominent role in the band, communication broke down and the inevitable happened – Lou was all but driven to quit.

After a hiatus spent living back with his parents on Long Island and working as a typist in the family business, Lou returned with the expected solo debut, *Lou Reed*, in 1972, an underwhelming, soft rock album featuring a bunch of songs left over from recent Velvet Underground rehearsals and sessions. It was also during this time that he met Bettye Kronstadt, a middle-class Jewish Long Island girl, while shopping in a department store. A quick romance bloomed with the waitress and aspiring actress and in next to no time, they had married, much to the delight of Lou's family. On what she was like as a person, Lou told *Fusion* magazine: "Bettye is not hip at all and I want to keep her that way. I believe in pretty princesses." It seemed Lou was trying to go straight in every sense.

But then he met David Bowie and everything went topsy-turvy again. The fruits of this meeting would see Lou change rock history for a second time. *Transformer*, 1972's glam 'n' glitter gender-bending androgynous sloppy-pop masterpiece, was co-produced by Bowie with Mick Ronson and aside from spawning the massive hit single 'Walk On the Wild Side', an effortlessly jazzy homage to the ghoulish and garish characters that populated Warhol's Factory during its heyday, *Transformer* also, for the first time, brought Lou the commercial success he had so desperately craved.

At home, things were not so good. His marriage to Bettye was on the rocks, a scenario that led her to attempt suicide while he was on tour. "She tried to commit suicide in a bathtub in the hotel," he later recalled. "It was someone standing there holding a razor blade. She looks like she might kill you but instead she starts cutting away at her wrists and there's blood everywhere. She lived but we had

to have a roadie there with her from then on." The disintegration of Lou's marriage to Bettye became the inspiration for *Berlin*, a druggy, bummed out, sleazy mini-opera about two hopelessly destructive lovers.

The album, released in 1973 was a critical bomb, earning Lou some of the worst reviews of his career. By autumn of that year, the marriage had bombed too and he and Bettye were divorced. All that year, he sought refuge in touring, staying on the road, trapped inside a self-destructive permanent haze of drug abuse.

Out of the tour came the massively successful live album, *Rock 'N' Roll Animal* followed by a new studio record, the laidback, druggy swagger of *Sally Can't Dance*, another huge commercial success. It seemed Lou could no wrong. Three albums on the trot, all hits. Going for broke, he opted for another live album, *Lou Reed Live,* in early 1975. Meanwhile, off-stage, Lou met a new muse and romantic partner: a half-Mexican Indian drag queen called Rachel: "It was in a late night club in Greenwich Village. I'd been up for days as usual and everything was at the

superreal glowing stage. I walked in and there was this amazing person, this incredible head kind of vibrating out of it all. Rachel was wearing this incredible make-up and dress and was absolutely in a different world to anyone in the place. Eventually I spoke and she came home with me." For the next couple of years, Lou and Rachel would be inseparable, him/her his inspiration, nurse, psychic bodyguard and partner. In a position where the record label would basically afford him to anything, he made full use of that artistic indulgence and dumped *Metal Machine Music*, a double album of speed-crazed industrial tonal sound on his record label's desk. After much freaking out on their part, it was released to abhorrent reviews and virtually no sales whatsoever. Lou had overnight blown a giant hole in his only recently untouchable career. He apologised to both fans and label with a very radio friendly new studio album, *Coney Island Baby*, a record characterised by laidback soft-rock grooves, full of love songs to Rachel.

INTRODUCTION

Wooed by Clive Davis to Arista, Lou's 1976 debut for the new label, *Rock And Roll Heart,* was met with a lukewarm reception, mainly because punk was breaking overground, spilling out from CBGB's. Reacting to what was going on down at the Bowery, Lou took a swing at the emerging punk scene with 1978's *Street Hassle*, a low down dirty album, full of street realism and boasting a cameo from rising star Bruce Springsteen. Off-stage, by early 1978, Lou and Rachel had split. Drinking and taking astonishing amounts of drugs, Lou delivered a season of belligerent and brilliant shows at The Bottom Line, taping the shows, to create *Take No Prisoners*, a hilarious live album full of ravings, monologues and ad-libs, Lou doing his best approximation of a Lenny Bruce stand-up routine. *The Bells*, released in 1979, was another inspired album that got great reviews, but sold poorly. Immersed in a toxic chemical lifestyle, Lou knew it was time for the party to stop. But he needed a helping hand to save him from drowning. The catalyst was Sylvia Morales, a twenty-two-year-old

stripper, part-time dominatrix and CBGBs habituee, who Lou first met in late 1978 at a meeting of the Eulenspiegel Society. By 1979, the two were living together, dividing their time between Lou's apartment in the city and a house they had bought in the rural suburb of Blairstown, New Jersey.

In 1980 they married on Valentine's Day and Lou's love for Sylvia dominated *Growing Up In Public*, a mixed bag of an album, released the same year. Under her powerful, healing influence, Lou quit drugs and alcohol for good and took up Wu-style tai chi chuan and Alcoholics Anonymous meetings. The turmoil of getting off all substances resulted in the 1982's furious cathartic album, *The Blue Mask*, which showcased Lou's new lead guitarist, former Voidoids axeman, Robert Quine. 1983 saw the release of *Legendary*

Hearts, another vehicle for the chiming, mangled Lou-Quine guitar partnership. However, re-runs of the Lou-Cale ego clashes soon spoiled the Lou-Quine sparring and *Live In Italy*, a dull live album that tried to emulate the success of *Rock 'N' Roll Animal,* turned out to be a swansong for the great Lou-Quine era. As happy married life rolled on, critics grumbled about a softening of the Lou muse, noting that *New Sensations* (1984) and *Mistrial* (1986), possessed synths, slick pop and rock tunes, but little in the way of depth. Genuine uproar from Lou's older fans surfaced with his endorsement of Honda scooters in a series of high profile ads. It seemed that with the onset of middle age, he had embraced the mainstream with open arms.

It took Andy Warhol's death in 1987 to reignite the old Lou muse and kickstart a renaissance in his songwriting. Soon after Warhol passed away, Lou and John Cale met up, agreed to work together again and in 1988, conceived the memorial song-cycle tribute to Warhol, *Songs For Drella,* for performance at the Brooklyn Academy of Music. This reigniting of the old partnership opened the door for the material to eventually become an album of the same name released in 1990. Creatively on a roll, in 1989 Lou unveiled the universally acclaimed album, *New York*, which spoke vividly and urgently of contemporary New York City. It seemed Lou had once more found the pulse again and was once more at the top of his game. The icing on the cake came in 1990 when the Cartier Foundation approached Sylvia (long since Lou's manager as well as wife) and asked her to ask Lou if the Velvet Underground would consider reforming for a one-off concert to inaugurate the Foundation's Andy Warhol retrospective. To everyone's amazement, a full band reunion took place in Paris on June 15th 1990.

Lou's golden age continued with 1992's *Magic And Loss*, a dark, intense album consumed with the death of two close friends. Meanwhile, the Cartier Foundation one-off had sparked inter-band discussions and in 1993, The Velvet Underground took off on a full-blown reunion tour, which started out promisingly, amicably, but ended somewhat predictably with Lou and the others barely speaking, Cale and Lou once more at each other's throats. Also in 1993, Lou had his essays and lyrics published under the title *Between Thought And Expression*. But all was not well at home.

INTRODUCTION

LOU REED *Talking*

By 1994, Lou and Sylvia were in the throes of separation and divorce and Lou was dating a new woman. This time he had fallen in love with the performance artist and musician, Laurie Anderson.

In 1995, Lou fulfilled a lifelong dream and stepped out in front of the camera, to make a cameo appearance in Wayne Wang's film *Blue In The Face*. The collaboration proved so successful, that when *Blue In Face* screenwriter Paul Auster made his directorial debut, *Lulu On The Bridge*, in 1998, he again wrote a cameo role especially for Lou. Meantime, he and Laurie Anderson had become seriously involved and were now living together. Just as *Lou Reed* had been dedicated to Bettye, *Coney Island Baby* to Rachel and *Growing Up In Public* to Sylvia, logically, his next album, *Set The Twilight Reeling* (1996), was one long love letter to Laurie Anderson.

Meanwhile, on 17 January 1996, The Velvet Underground were inducted into The Rock And Roll Hall Of Fame, though sadly by then, both Nico and Sterling Morrison had passed away. Under pressure to deliver a strong selling record, Lou followed *Set The Twilight Reeling* with the tried and tested live album formula, releasing *Perfect Night live* in 1998.

Then, in 2000, he returned with *Ecstasy*, a terrific hard rocking, libido tribunal and saw his collected lyrics published as *Pass Thru Fire*. Working again with Robert Wilson throughout 2001, Lou scored *Timerocker*. Earlier, he and Lou had collaborated on *POEtry* in 1996, a tribute to the poetry of Edgar Allan Poe.

In 2002, to everyone's surprise, Lou stormed the singles charts with a DJ remix of 'Satellite Of Love' and published a monograph of his photographs, *Emotion in Action*. Keeping a keen pace going, he released *The Raven* in 2003, a spoken word-music album that gave Lou a chance to once again celebrate Edgar Allen Poe's poetry. In 2004, he unleashed yet another live album, *Animal Serenade* before parting company with Warner Bros.

Today, Lou Reed holds a powerful, pioneering position in rock history. Always busy with music, photography or film projects, he's set to return with a new studio album in 2006, the first fruits of a new multi-album deal with Sanctuary Records. He's still with Laurie Anderson – the couple share a loft space in the Meat Packing District in Manhattan. Their close friends include fellow like-minded artists such as Salman Rushdie, Paul Auster, Julian Schnabel and Bono. He's super-fit these days, preferring Tai Chi to amphetamines. Lou Reed might be in his sixties but he's as driven as ever and has no intention of slowing down or stopping work.

"I was just reading the biography of Katharine Hepburn", he quipped in early 2005. "To age 96 she would just keep working, working, working, working. And that's what Warhol said. And most of the people I know, that's all they do."

INTRODUCTION

The Early Years

"My parents were self-made millionaires. On paper they were very rich. I know what it's like to have money. They would love me to take over their companies. It's tax law – it all has to do with numbers. If United Steel is your client you can save them millions." 1976

"I used to love algebra. I liked it because it was so logical. You could make up your own theorems and still have it work out. I like that kind of math. It ends the chaos."

2000

"I started classical piano when I was a tot – eight, ten, something like that. I just had a natural affinity for music." 1976

"I got a guitar, a Gretsch Country Gentleman and I paid somebody to teach me those first three chords. After that you're on your own, particularly at a time when you could play everything on the radio with those three chords." 1982

LOU REED *Talking*

❝I always loved guitars and rock and roll. Who didn't? All through college and high school, for that matter, I was in bands playing in bars. We played the Top 10, Top 40, whatever was popular then, that's what we played.**❞** 1998

❝I resent it. It was a very big drag. From age twelve on I could have been having a ball and not even thought about this shit. What a waste of time. If the forbidden thing is love, then you spend most of your time playing with hate. Who needs that? I feel I was gypped.❞ ON FIRST HOMOSEXUAL FEELINGS 1979

❝There's a 45 I made when I was fourteen. I'm in the background, playing guitar and going 'ooh'. It was just three of us. I played guitar. I didn't sing. I wrote the material, but the material was just a mimic of what was on the radio. That was doomed to failure. That was the first professional recording I made. It was kind of fantastic. King Curtis, the saxophonist, was on it. And I was not really aware of who King Curtis was at the time.**❞** 1998

❝I think that the earlier you know, the bigger jump you have on absolutely everybody else. It's a big advantage because you do pick up things along the way. If you have a five year jump on somebody, that's a five year jump. What's an all-purpose microphone? What's an automatic level control? What headphones aren't going to dissolve in front of you? What machine won't blow up? You see, I didn't study music, I just learned in a bar. I started out on classical piano but I dropped. On the day I heard rock, that was the end of it. I made my first record when I was fourteen. I lived in bars, all through high school, all through college. I was always the youngest then. So none of this other stuff is any big deal to me. So that's my background, even though I have a BA in English. But I was just a guitar player. I didn't move to the front for a while. That took conniving. To get to the front, I had to write the stuff. That was the only way I would get up there, because it wouldn't be the sound of my voice that would accomplish that one.❞ 2002

 **LOU REED** *Talking*

On College

"I can't even remember going to college.**"** 2003

"I didn't care for the academic life at all. That's not to put it down – some people love it. But I didn't." 1982

"I always wanted to be a writer and I went to college to prepare myself for it. See, that's where I'm coming from. If you have my interests and my kind of academic background, then what I'm doing is not really an unlikely thing to do." 1982

"I'm an English major. I had one of those useless degrees." 2004

"I kept writing little things on my own when I was in school at Syracuse University, studying with Delmore Schwartz, reading George Eliot, Phillip Booth, people like that, in creative-writing courses, poetry courses. So that's kind of my background. I was doing that and bar bands. Really bad ones." 1998

"Delmore Schwartz was the unhappiest man who I ever met in my life and the smartest – till I met Andy Warhol. He didn't use curse words until he was thirty. His mother wouldn't allow him. His worst fears were realised when he died and they put him in a plot next to her. Once, drunk in a Syracuse bar, he said, If you sell out Lou, I'm gonna' get ya. I hadn't thought about doing anything, let alone selling out. Two years later, he was gone." 1978

"I was certainly into William Burroughs and Allen Ginsberg. But also I studied with Delmore Schwartz and I worshipped him. I was a fan of Hubert Selby and Raymond Chandler and a big fan of doo-wop. So that's the amalgam." 2004

"I have always been reading Raymond Chandler. The things he could do with simple words! Fabulous. Many good poets have inspired me: Hubert Selby Jr., William Burroughs, Allen Ginsberg. People who write simple and to the point. Who don't use difficult words." 2005

"I was enamored of R&B like practically everybody else I know. Just worshipping that kind of playing and singing. There wasn't really any alternative stuff going on lyrically. Everybody cites Little Richard. There was nothing quite like hearing 'Long Tall Sally' for the first time." 2004

ON COLLEGE

The Graduate

"I got it off a mashed-in Negro whose features were in two sections named Jaw." ON CONTRACTING HEPATITIS AFTER GRADUATION 1970

"The Beatles were innocent of the world and its wicked ways while I no longer possessed this pristine view. I, after all, had had jaundice.**"** 1972

"I wasn't applying for a job at *The New Yorker*. I didn't have any plan. The extent of my plan was not to get drafted into the Vietnam War." 2004

"I said I wanted a gun and would shoot anyone or anything in front of me. I was pronounced mentally unfit.**"**

ON GETTING OUT OF THE DRAFT 1972

"*The New Yorker* rejected me. That's when I wanted to be a New Yorker poet. I used to get *Writer's Market* which told you all the books that take poetry like *The Kenyon Review, Hudson Review, Paris Review*, but later it dawned on me, who wants to be published in these magazines, anyway?" 1974

"I got a job when I got out of school at a budget-record line, Pickwick Records. And we would write real hack stuff. If surfing was popular, we would write ten surfing songs and make up the names of the groups. But it was really just me and three other guys. And they'd sell these albums for a buck in Woolworth's." 1998

"We just churned out songs, that's all. Never a hit song. What we were doing was churning out these ripoff albums. In other words, the album would say it featured four groups and it wouldn't really be four groups, it would just be various permutations of us and they would sell them at supermarkets for 99 cents or a dollar. While I was doing that I was doing my own stuff and trying to get by but the material I was doing, people wouldn't go near me with it at the time." 1972

"I wrote penny tunes. They were 99 cents for each record. We imitated the big hits of the day. So if, say, they wanted Detroit, we wrote Detroit. No, it was worse than that. It was just the worst possible thing you could imagine." 2004

"I wrote for a company where it was nothing but copies of copies of copies. Whatever was pop. I was hired as a staff song writer - hired is barely the word - for a label that produced records sold for $1. Long-playing records, whatever was popular. If songs were popular about cars, we would have an album of songs by make-believe groups about cars. That was it. They would sell for 99 cents in department stores. Yes, write four death songs; write some surfing songs. That's what I did. I did it for almost a year, I was learning how to use this studio, because you had to record immediately. Boom! In. Out. We're talking about junk! I sang some of them. But it would all be made-up groups like The Beach Nuts. Or Wave Bunnies or Sand Demons. You know, just trying to cash in. I learned to write quickly, that's for sure. What are you doing? Write another song! Okay boom! There you go. It was easy."

2004

"If you're reading Selby and Burroughs and Ginsberg, you just think, my God, imagine putting this stuff to guitars and drums. Wow, wouldn't that be something? It's such a simple idea it's almost not worth commenting on." 2004

THE GRADUATE

The Velvet Underground

❝The Primitives was a made up group. The Ostrich guitar was a guitar I used on a record called 'The Ostrich' - all the strings were tuned to one note.❞ 1993

❝One day a guy at Pickwick showed me a trick - he tuned all the strings on the guitar to one note. He was kidding around but I thought it was amazing. So I did it and then I turned the amplifier loud, it was feeding back and it had to be in key because it's all one note. And then one day, while we were there recording our 20 surfing or death songs, I made up a song called 'The Ostrich'. And they thought that this one could actually be a real record. They needed other members to say it was a group and that's when we found John Cale.❞ 2002

❝When I first met Lou Reed at the beginning of 1965, he was a twenty-two-year-old songwriter at Pickwick Records in Long Island and I was a twenty-two-year-old avant garde classical musican in LaMonte Young's Theater of Eternal Music. We were introduced by a Pickwick producer, Terry Phillips, who thought I was a pop musician because I had long hair. He asked me, Tony Conrad and a friend, the sculptor Walter de Maria, to form a band with Lou called The Primitives. Phillips wanted to publicise a song Lou had written and recorded in a back room and Pickwick had released as a single, 'The Ostrich', by a fictitious band, The Primitives.❞ JOHN CALE, 1999

"Being friends with Lou put me in touch with the outside world. Working with LaMonte Young was just abstration, like being in a monastery. But with Lou, it was like suddenly the street was right there in my face. It was very interesting. Especially the lingo. After working with LaMonte on the music and esoteric theories, what really grabbed me was that I was dealing with the English language again. I don't mean in the way that Lou was writing but what he introduced me to and what I saw while I was running around with him. It was this world of conversation and lingo. Lou was running the hustler scene, it was like a parade of extraordinary characters. And this continued at the Factory.**"** JOHN CALE, 1998

"My first impressions of Lou were of a high-strung, intelligent fragile college kid in a polo neck sweater, rumpled jeans and loafers. He had been around and was bruised, trembling, quiet and insecure. He lived in Freeport, Long Island, with his parents, who kept him on a tight rein. In fact, he was only allowed to come into Manhattan on the weekend, for the rest of the week he was grounded. He was also seeing a psychiatrist who prescribed a tranquiliser called Placidyl. When I asked why, he said, 'I think I'm crazy'. I told him, 'Fuck you're not crazy'."

JOHN CALE, 1999

JOHN CALE

"To me, Lou was the kind of person who would survive in New York and I wanted to learn from him.**"** JOHN CALE, 1998

THE VELVET UNDERGROUND **"**

"There's a certain level of understanding that you have to have about Lou. When I met him, he was just coming out of shock treatments. His parents had decided that the way to deal with his problems, a gay life, whatever, was to give him shock therapy and no way can you not see that as barbaric. And he was out to make sure that everybody knew about it and that everybody paid for it. So I understand that. It was something that he had been through against his will and it was something that I was interested in going through as an experience. I was applying for sensory deprivation programmes at NYU and at Columbia University and at MIT. Professors were getting letters from me saying, Can I be put in a tank for forty eight hours? I was watching everything going on. I was reading everything the austronauts were reading and every pill they took and when they took it. It was a wonderful life." 1998

"I only hope that one day John will be recognised as the Beethoven of his day. He knows so much about music, he's such a great musician. He's completely mad. But that's because he's Welsh." 1969

"Lou was a lot of fun. He enjoyed taking situations to extremes you couldn't imagine until you'd been there with him. He would befriend a drunk in a bar and after drawing him out with friendly conversation, suddenly ask, 'Would you like to fuck your mother?'" JOHN CALE, 1999

"Lou enjoyed getting drunk and taking Placidyls."

JOHN CALE, 1999

VELVET UNDERGROUND: NICO, MO TUCKER. STERLING MORRISON, LOU AND JOHN CALE

"Then I ran into Sterling Morrison on the subway. We needed a drummer and his friend Jim Tucker had a sister named Maureen who loved to play drums and had a car, and that was it: The Velvet Underground. It's weird the way things work." 2002

"Was there any plan? Was there any goal? Not really, just playing. And three out of four of us were college graduates of all things. One of us was even here on the Leonard Bernstein Scholarship. So, it's a weird conglomeration. Sterling was going for his M.A. in Classical English Literature. And there we were. We played these dives like no one else. While I was writing this crappy stuff, I was also writing my own stuff. Why? I don't know why. Did I hope to get recorded? No. I was just writing. That's what I have been doing since I was nine. I had read somewhere that ostrich feathers were supposed to be popular, so I wrote a song called 'The Ostrich'. The feedback made the people at radio stations think the record was defective and they sent it back. That was the end of it, but by then we had become a band called The Velvet Underground." 2002

THE VELVET UNDERGROUND

"We used to have a rule. Anyone who plays a blues riff gets fined five dollars." 2004

"We didn't want to do derivative blues. We were very aware of that. That's not what we were about. I couldn't play it either so that was another good reason to stay away from it. There were people who could really, really play that well, and I couldn't. I think of the Velvets' work as realistic, not bleak. You're talking to somebody who was around Warhol, and also reading Allen Ginsberg and *Naked Lunch* and *Junkie* by William Burroughs. I can't compare myself to them. I wouldn't dream of it, but some of the subject matter may bear a similarity." 1998

"The only things we had in common were drugs and an obsession with risk taking. That was the raison d'etre for The Velvet Underground." JOHN CALE, 1999

"Maureen Tucker's so beautiful. She has to be one of the most fantastic people I've ever met in my life. She's so impossibly great." 1968

"Our first gig (in November 1965), we were so loud and horrifying to the high school audience that the majority of them, teachers, students and parents, fled screaming." JOHN CALE, 1998

"I just tried to find a chord that would work on all his chords. He could play D, G and E and I'd have two fewer. I'd have one chord that would go through it. That worked. That's how we did 'Heroin' and 'Venus In Furs'. In my mind, I was trying to find the one thing that would set us apart from other bands. I did a lot of little things. We didn't tune our guitars the same way as everybody else. We went down a whole tone and gradually all this stuff from LaMonte Young crept into the structure of everything. And I wanted to do something particular, so that nobody could come around the corner and just pick up whatever we were doing and just do it. It took about a year to get to that point. But when it happened it was unique, it wasn't just intonation, it was really sizzling, what we stood for and the arrangements." JOHN CALE, 1998

"The basic idea was that the music should always match the lyrics. 'Heroin' is a perfect example. So is 'Venus In Furs' and 'All Tomorrow's Parties'. The same idea runs through every song I've ever written. But we were having fun. You must understand that we weren't critics, only players. Players play and they don't sit around assessing it. At least this one doesn't. We certainly did enjoy what we were doing and we were very pure. One hundred per cent devoted to music as music, without any other considerations. That's why it was great to be picked up by Warhol, who loved us just the way we were and didn't try to change anything except, you know, give us a chanteuse. I guess he thought we needed someone who was really good looking."

2005

THE VELVETS, WITH MEMBERS OF ANDY
WARHOL'S FACTORY AND ANDY (CENTRE)

THE VELVET UNDERGROUND

❝ My God, what luck was that - of all the people to adopt you as his band. It was fantastic. He did it all, we played the same music we had been fired for and beaten up elsewhere. The first week he projected films onto us and we wore black: that was the first multimedia show. People hated him, but now he's dead, he's maybe the greatest American artist. **❞** 2003

ANDY WARHOL

❝ We couldn't get jobs anywhere, but we had this material, and eventually we played a dive. Once, somebody brought Andy Warhol in, and the next thing you know, he said, I have a week at the Cinematheque. Oh, I don't know what to do. I have a week. What shall I do? Oh, I know. You'll play, and I'll show movies. We'll get lights. So I said, Okay, fine. Then it went from there. Andy adopted us. ❞ 2002

❝ The first thing I liked about Andy was that he was very real. **❞** 1987

❝ Lou was very suspicious of Andy Warhol but on the other hand, he was in awe of him. ❞ JOHN CALE, 1999

❝ The first time we played a show in New York was at a place called the Café Bizarre. It was just a tourist place, there were no people there. After that, Jonas Mekas, who now has the Anthology Film Archives, had a place called the Cinemathèque. Andy Warhol had a week at the Cinemathèque, and he decided to show his movies on us while we played and Andy was interviewing the audience. No one'd ever seen anything like it before. **❞** 1998

"We would stand there on stage, dressed all in black, with black glasses and he would project movies onto us – slides and films – and we would stand there and play. He was a genius. I often ask myself when I'm writing something or working on something, 'What would Andy do?'" 2004

"Andy wanted us to use Nico and we went along with it at the time. We didn't really feel we needed a chanteuse, but Andy asked me to write a song about Edie Sedgwick, so I did and called it 'Femme Fatale' and we gave it to Nico because she could sing the high chorus. That's why at the end of the song, you get those oh-woa-woas, with all due respect to Nico." 1987

"Nico's the kind of person that you meet and you're not quite the same afterwards. She has an amazing mind. She isn't the type of person who stays very long in any one country. Nico's fantastic. She always understood immediately what I was after with a song." 1972

"I wrote some songs just for Nico. And she had that great deep voice. I hate the sound of my voice on tape. When I hear my voice I only hear wrong." 2004

NICO

"In our show the guy who was doing the lights, Danny Williams, he committed suicide eventually. He would sit up for hours at the Factory with seven strobe lights and use himself as a test subject. That's why John and I used to wear sunglasses when we played. We didn't want to see it." 1976

THE VELVET UNDERGROUND

LOU REED *Talking*

“We play in the dark so that the music's just there.” 1966

“**Everybody at the factory adored Lou.**” JOHN CALE, 1998

“Our music's for the pretty people, all the beautiful people.” 1966

“**Andy told me that what we were doing with music was the same thing he was doing with paintings and movies, ie not kidding around. To my mind nobody in music was doing anything that even approximated the real thing, with the exception of us. We were doing a specific thing that was very, very real. It wasn't slick or a lie in any conceivable way which was the only way we could work with him.**” 1987

“The only jobs we had were when somebody would ask Warhol to show his things in a museum or in a film festival at a college and he would take us. The Chrysler Museum would invite him and we would go and play in the museum, which would be showing slides and movies on top of us while we played.” 1998

“**We're attacked constantly. No one ever writes anything nice about us. You get tired of being called obscene.**” 1966

“All the songs for the first Velvet Underground album were written before I ever met Andy. It's just that they happened to match Andy's thing perfectly.” 1976

“**All that meant was that he believed in us and he would prevent the engineers from messing with it. Andy would say, 'Don't touch it. Leave it alone. Leave it just like that.' And these engineers would want to add all this other stuff but he wouldn't allow it.**”
ON WARHOL'S ROLE IN PRODUCING THE VELVET UNDERGROUND AND NICO 2004

“I was very taken aback when people were surprised when The Velvet Underground consciously set out to put themes common to movies, plays and novels into a pop song format.” 1982

"There are songs that Lou wrote that still blow my mind."

MO TUCKER, 1997

"Some people get a kick out of architecture. You know, they build a bridge or a house or a this or a that. I like playing rock and roll and playing with the lyrics. I never compared our music to Pop Art, although the movies Andy was making were like the songs or the songs were like the movies, and they were both unlike anything else that was around right then. It was the alternative to Hollywood and pop. Warhol gave us a home, so to speak. Certainly that made it possible to feel encouragement to keep going in this direction. It fit like a hand in a glove. I can't imagine any other group that could've been there with him. We were incredibly lucky. No one knew or cared about us but he took us seriously. Otherwise, we were unemployable." **1998**

"So Nico photographs well in black and white. I'm not playing with her anymore." 1967

"Everybody wanted to be the star. Of course Lou always was. But the newspapers came to me all the time. That's how I got fired – he couldn't take that anymore." **NICO, 1978**

"I fired Warhol. He said to me, 'Aren't you tired of playing museums?' I thought about it and fired him. I was just trying to do what Andy suggested." 1968

"The crunch came when we were getting ready to go to Cleveland in September 1968. Lou met Mo and Sterling in a restaurant in Sheridan Square and said, 'If Cale goes to Cleveland, I don't go.' That was it. We had got to the end of our tether." **JOHN CALE, 1999**

"I left because the music was turning redundant, we weren't much working on the music anymore – and I decided I was going to find another career." JOHN CALE, 1998

THE VELVET UNDERGROUND

❝Sterling showed up at my apartment and effectively told me that I was no longer in the band. Lou always got other people to do his dirty work for him.❞ **JOHN CALE 1972**

DINNER WITH ANDY WARHOL

❝Lou likes a collaborator or facilitator, someone who will help him through because he's minimally musical. He's really made a career out of using his inadequacies creatively. Which is not a bad thing, it's a good thing to do. But he's not real strong on music. He's not a real strong guitar player in the sense of technique or anything like that. He's real strong in terms of will. I will turn this guitar up. And I will thrash it. And I will dominate this situation.❞ DOUG YULE, 1995

❝We would spend time together, where he would take out these songs that he was fooling around with and ask for help: I'm thinking about this melody, what's a chord that goes with that? He'd ask for help building things then he would return six months later with the song put together and announce it: here's my new tune.❞ **DOUG YULE 1995**

"There were a lot of things going on that summer. Internally, within the band, the situation, the milieu, and especially the management. Situations that could only be solved by as abrupt a departure as possible once I had made the decision. I just walked out because we didn't have any money, I didn't want to tour again – I can't get any writing done on tour and the grind is terrible – and I'd wondered for a long time if we were ever going to be accepted on a large scale. Words can't do justice to the way I got worked over with the money.**"** 1971

"It was a process of elimination from the start. First no more Andy, then no more Nico, then no more John, then no more Velvet Underground.**"** 1978

"I'm proud of our legacy. We were there. We did it. We made some incredibly pure records. And there were great collaborations between me, John, Sterling, Mo and Dougie. We tried our very, very best and I think we accomplished some amazing things with those records.**"** 2000

THE VELVET UNDERGROUND **"**

The Velvet Underground Albums

The Velvet Underground And Nico (1967)

"Andy did a photograph of a banana for the album cover and now I've just seen a blow-up of a banana and it's really gotten huge and enveloped all other types of significance as a banana. It's an extremely pretty sexy banana and the album cover peels which is nice, to reveal the inside of a very sexy, groovy banana." 1966

"Andy said I should write a song about Edie Sedgwick. I said, 'Like what?' and he said, 'Oh, don't you think she's a femme fatale, Lou?' So I wrote 'Femme Fatale' and we gave it to Nico." 1966

"We were trying to a Phil Spector thing with as few instruments as possible." JOHN CALE, 1980

"Lou was paranoid and eventually he made everybody paranoid."
JOHN CALE, 1970

"The whole time the album was being made, nobody seemed happy with it." ANDY WARHOL, 1969

LOU REED *Talking*

❝I checked myself out of the hospital to go to Delmore's funeral and never went back.❞
ON CONTRACTING HEPATITIS (IN 1966), 1972

❝Andy made a point of trying to make sure that on our first album the language remained intact. He would say, 'Make sure you do the song with the dirty words, don't change the words just because it's a record.'❞ **1972**

❝We wrote 'Femme Fatale' about somebody who was one and has since been committed to an institution for being one. And will one day open up a school to train others.❞ 1967

White Light / White Heat (1968)

❝The second album was like hanging by your fingerrnails.❞

JOHN CALE 1978

❝When we did 'Sister Ray' we turned up to ten flat out, leakage all over the place.❞ JOHN CALE, 1968

❝The only way to go through something is to go right into the middle, the only way to do it is to not kid around. Storm coming, you go right through the center.❞ **1970**

❝We were doing the whole heavy metal trip back then. I mean if 'Sister Ray' is not an example of heavy metal, then nothing is.❞

1972

The Velvet Underground (1969)

"I've gotten to where I like the pretty stuff better than drive and distortion because you can be more subtle, really say something and sort of soothe." 1969

"All our effect boxes were locked in a munitions box that was stolen at the airport when we were leaving for the West Coast to record. We saw that all our tricks had vanished and instead of trying to replace them we just thought we could do without them." STERLING MORRISON, 1970

"This song would follow this song because this has to do with this and this has to do with that and this will answer that and then you've got this character who matches this character or offsets this character. The third album was really the quintessence of that idea because it started out with 'Candy Says' where this girl asks all these questions." 1969

"I was working with Doug Yule's innocence. I'm sure he never understood a word of what he was singing. He doesn't know what it's about." 1972

Loaded (1970)

"Maureen was pregnant at the time with her first child and Sterling became discouraged early on because he felt I had too much an influence in it, he felt basically, sort of cut out, which I'm sure a lot of it has to do with the fact that I was feeling much more confident since the third album, more a part of the group. Also Lou leaned on me a lot in terms of musical support and for harmonies, vocal arrangements. I did a lot on *Loaded*. It sort of evolved down to the Lou and Doug recreational recording." **DOUG YULE, 1995**

THE VELVET UNDERGROUND ALBUMS

"I gave them an album loaded with hits and it was loaded with hits to the point where the rest of the people showed their colours. So I left them to their album full of hits that I made." 1972

"For all intensive purposes it was in the can when Lou quit. I think the biggest change after Lou left was that Sesnick (the band's manager) rearranged the credits on the back of the album to make Lou look as insignificant as possible. I think he's listed below everyone else." DOUG YULE, 1995

The Velvet Underground Live at Max's Kansas City (1972)

"I hated playing at Max's because I couldn't do the songs I wanted to do and I was under a lot of pressure to do things I didn't want to do." 1972

1969 The Velvet Underground Live (1974)

"The 1969 tapes were recorded by the owners at the Matrix and End of Cole Ave. I don't like it because it was taped in small locations. Generally our sound was bigger. On this record everything is subdued, there are no really loud songs." STERLING MORRISON, 1969

V.U. (1984)

"Twenty years on, listening to The Velvet Underground is still like dancing with lightning. It would take considerably more space than we could conveniently devote here to fully describe the totality of their impact and influence upon successive generations of aspiring young hipsters over the last two decades. V.U. cuts through most of the moment's crap like razor with its blade on fire, even though most of the tracks included on this retrospective compilation will already be familiar to the dedicated Velvets fanatic who will have hunted down the majority of them over the years on a variety of bootlegs. These people will, of course, identify more than half of the ten songs that Lou Reed subsequently re-worked during the course of his solo career. I can only hope that these people agree with me when I suggest that all of these original blueprints outstrip their later incarnation, mostly by immeasurable distances."

ALLAN JONES, *MELODY MAKER*, 1985

THE VELVET UNDERGROUND ALBUMS

Two Relationships

On Bettye

66 My marriage (to Bettye), it was kind of a pessimistic act – nothing else to do at the time. 99 1974

66 **She was a secretary when one was needed at the time.** 99 1975

66 During the *Berlin* sessions, my old lady who was an asshole but I needed a female asshole around to bolster me up, I needed a sycophant who could bounce around and she fit the bill, but she called it love, ha! She tried to commit suicide in the bathtub at the hotel. Cut her wrists – she lived. But we had to have a roadie there with her from then on. 99 1978

66 **Everyone should have a divorce once, I can recommend it. All the money I make, she gets. Now I don't get headaches anymore and I'm poorer.** 99 ON DIVORCING BETTYE 1973

On Rachel

"She's a he." 1975

"Rachel knows how to do it for me. No one else ever did before. Rachel's something else." 1976

"I enjoy being around Rachel, that's all there is to it. Whatever it is I need, Rachel seems to supply it." 1976

"Rachel is very interesting. Doesn't react very much but full of great quotes. The other day it was, 'If you're gonna' be black be black but don't give me no shades of grey.'" 1976

"Rachel's a street kid and very tough underneath it all." 1976

"Rachel has looked after the money and kept me in shape and watched over the road crew. At last there's someone hustling around for me that I can trust."

1976

TWO RELATIONSHIPS "

Solo In The Seventies

❝I was a typist for two years in the family business. My mother always told me in high school, You should take typing, it gives you something to fall back on. She was right.❞ 1976

THE ALBUMS

Lou Reed (1972)

❝A lot of what I do is intuitive. I just go where it takes me and I don't question it.❞ 1971

❝I'm not consulting anybody this time. It's a solo effort with my producer Richard Robinson.❞ 1971

❝There's just too many things wrong with it. I was in dandy form and so was everybody else. I'm just aware of all the things that are missing and all the things that shouldn't have been there.❞

1972

Transformer (1972)

❝The people I was around at the time thought Bowie would be the perfect producer for me to make a record that would sell. And it turned out to be totally true.❞ 1982

WITH DAVID BYRNE, PATTI SMITH AND JOHN CALE AT THE OCEAN CLUB JULY 1976

❝**David was a really smart guy. He and Mick Ronson were two of the few people who knew how to play that Velvets stuff. And, of course, when he produced me I had hits. 'Walk On The Wild Side' paid the bills for years, so I've loved David forever for that.**❞ 2004

❝Andy once just told me to write a song called 'Vicious'. So I did.❞

2004

❝**Last time they were all love songs, this time they're all hate songs.**❞ 1972

SOLO IN THE SEVENTIES

❝The gay life at the moment isn't that great. I wanted to write a song which made it terrific, something that you'd enjoy.❞

ON 'MAKE UP' 1972

❝Just because you're gay doesn't mean you have to camp around in make up. The make up thing is just a style thing now. If people have homosexuality in them, it won't necessarily involve make up in the first place.❞ ON 'MAKE UP' 1973

❝The first time he ever conceived of the song 'Satellite Of Love', he was thinking of it, he was in a limousine. He, me and Sesnick were riding in a limo and he was talking about someone had just launched a satellite. I forget what it was, he was riffing off that idea and conceiving of this song and tying it back into songs about love. Because that's what always sells and that's literally where it came from. It was designed in his mind as a hit and that's what he was looking for: a hit.❞ **DOUG YULE, 1995**

Berlin (1973)

❝I don't have a clue where it came from. I had met (producer) Bob Ezrin and we decided to work together. And I had the idea for the songs and Bob said, 'Wow, it could be a movie for the mind'. We had a little plot going on there. Boy meets girl, boy gets girl, boy loses girl and that's when it ends. We left out the last step because that was always the way it went in my life. You always have the happy ending. So we thought, 'Let's not have that. That's not happening to me. How about you Bob?' And he brought in arrangers and players. It was an amazing album. But a bitch. That album caused grief for both of us. It had repercussions. Some times you do these things and they're alive. They don't just sit over there. They reverberate through your own personal life.❞

2000

"Berlin is a divided city and a lot of potentially violent things go on there. And it's not America although some of the characters appear to be American. It just seemed better than calling it Omaha. Berlin was just suggestive to me. It makes it tackier that it's in Berlin – it reminds me of Von Stroheim and Dietrich." 1973

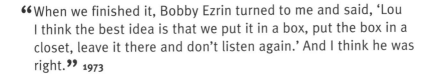

"It's involved with violence both mental and physical. It takes place for real in Berlin 1973. The really important thing is the relationship between the two major characters. The narrator is filling you in from his point of view and his point of view is not particularly pleasant." 1973

"When we finished it, Bobby Ezrin turned to me and said, 'Lou I think the best idea is that we put it in a box, put the box in a closet, leave it there and don't listen again.' And I think he was right." 1973

"We killed ourselves psychologically on that album. We went so far into it that it was kinda hard to get out." 1976

"I had to do *Berlin*. If I hadn't done it, I'd have gone crazy. If I hadn't got it out of my hair, I would have exploded. It was a very painful album to make. I don't wanna go through it again, having to say those words over and over and over." 1974

"The way that album was overlooked was probably the biggest disappointment I ever faced. I pulled the blinds SHUT at that point. And they've remained closed." 1977

SOLO IN THE SEVENTIES

Rock 'N' Roll Animal (1974)

"It's the way those things should be done and hadn't been done correctly." 1974

Sally Can't Dance (1974)

"I slept through *Sally Can't Dance*. They'd make a suggestion and I'd say, 'Oh all right'. I'd do the vocals in one take, in twenty minutes and then it was goodbye." 1974

"I've been rewriting the same song for a long time. Except my bullshit is worth most people's diamonds. And diamonds are a girl's best friend. *Sally Can't Dance* is cheap and tedious. It was produced in the slimiest way possible. I think it's shit. I like leakage. I wish all the Dolbys were just ripped outta the studio. I've spent more time getting rid of all that fucking shit. I like all the old Velvets records; I don't like Lou Reed records. I like *Berlin* and I positively LOVE *Metal Machine Music* because that's the idea I had years ago but I didn't have the money or machines to do it." 1976

"It's tedious. Could you imagine putting out *Sally Can't Dance* with your name on it? Dyeing my hair and all that shit? That's what they wanted, that's what they got. *Sally Can't Dance* went into the Top Ten without a single and I said, 'Ah what a piece of shit.'" 1975

"This is fantastic – the worse I am, the more it sells." 1974

"It's cheap and nasty." 1976

"I hate that album. I just can't write songs you can dance to." 1977

"I sound terrible but I was singing about the worst shit in the world. That wasn't a parody. That was what was happening." 1978

WITH R.C. KELLY FILMING A PROMOTIONAL VIDEO

LOU REED *Talking*

Lou Reed Live (1975)

❝Lou ended up doing album after album of reissues of the same song.❞ **JOHN CALE 1982**

Metal Machine Music (1975)

❝*Metal Machine Music* is probably one of the best things I ever did and I've been thinking about doing it ever since I've been listening to LaMonte Young. I had also been listening to Xenakis a lot. You know the drone thing? Well, doing it with a band, you always had to depend on other people. And inevitably you find that one person is stronger than another.❞ 1976

❝I did it like that (make each side 16:01 minutes long) because I wanted to cut it hot. And since you're dealing in certain types of distortion up to a certain level of harmonics, I had to have grooves as wide as possible because the closer they are, the lower your gain.❞ 1976

❝There was an information breakdown. They wanted to put it out on Red Seal and I said no, because that would have been pretentious. I wasn't going to put it out at all. But a friend of mine at another record company asked to hear it and said why don't you play it for this guy who was the head of classical music at RCA. I think *Metal Machine Music* got him fired. I played it for him and he loved it. I thought he must be mad but he said we really must put it out. He bypassed the A&R people there and went right to Glancy, said, 'We have to have it out on Red Seal'. I said no way. He said why. I said because it seems dilettantish and hypocritical like saying, 'The really smart, complicated stuff is over here, in the classical bin, meanwhile the shit rock 'n' roll goes over here where the shmucks are'. I said,' Fuck you, if you want it out, you put it out on the regular label with all the other stuff. All you do is put on a disclaimer'. Which didn't happen, unfortunately. In other words if a kid saw the cover where I'm standing with a microphone and said, 'Wow a live album!', they'd say, 'What a ripoff!' What they shoulda had was a disclaimer that said before you buy, listen to it for two minutes because you're not gonna like it and I said in the liner notes you're not gonna' like it.**❞** 1976

❝It was a giant fuck you but not the way you're saying it. The former head of Red Seal got me curious to see how it would hold up against LaMonte, Xenakis etc. And I think it held up well against them all, in fact far better. But I'm not interested in anybody's opinion except my own. When you say 'garage music', well, that's true to an untrained ear maybe but there's all kinds of symphonic ripoffs in there, running all through it, little pastoral parts, but they go by like bap!, in five seconds. Like Beethoven's Third or Mozart. You don't do that note for note symphonic thing by accident. I had the machines do it. It's very simple for anybody that knows what I'm talking about. Bach and Beethoven both wrote pieces that weren't supposed to be played by people. Now people play them and I'm sure if they were around now they'd be amazed but they'd also be playing with machines because nobody can play that thing. But you don't accidentally have part of the Glass harp in there. You don't accidentally have part of Eroica. They keep building up. The thing is you have to listen for it. But most people get stopped by the initial thing they hear, which is fine by me.**❞** 1976

SOLO IN THE SEVENTIES **❞**

"It took a couple of weeks (to record). I had amps and a tape recorder. I tuned the guitars a certain way to set up a feedback loop and then I was also playing with the speed of the tape recorder." 2000

"I set out to make a beautiful record and I happen to think I succeeded. I thought people would love it. I mean, if you're into guitar feedback and lots of it, if you're not so keen on melodies and rhythm, then it's the perfect record. What could be more fun? Okay everyone hated it at the time and I was told it would finish my career but look at the influence it's had. *Metal Machine Music* practically invented industrial rock. Did I always know it would prove to be so influential? I had no fucking idea." 2004

"I took a real beating over that. It was supposed to have a big thing on it saying, 'No lyrics No song No voice' but it didn't. It just said in the tiniest letters 'An electronic composition', so people ordered it under the mistaken impression that it was something else. So they had incredible returns. And the records stores said, 'We'll never buy any new record of yours again. Ever, ever, ever. This is a terrible thing'. People thought they were being misled, that if they wanted an instrumental album then they should have been told." 2000

"*Metal Machine Music* was made twenty-seven or twenty-eight years ago. In the year 2000 they re-released it with a new mastering job by me and Bob Ludwig: the 25th anniversary of *Metal Machine Music*. It was taken off the market three weeks after it was released. But time goes by and people get more used to what you call loops and electronics and noise and feedback." 2003

"Shovelling coal in a coal mine? That's work. Playing guitar? I don't call that work."

"You know the expression 'God protects fools and drunks'? I qualify for both."

"

"Andy once just told me to write a song called 'Vicious'. So I did."

"You're a musician: You play. That's what you do."

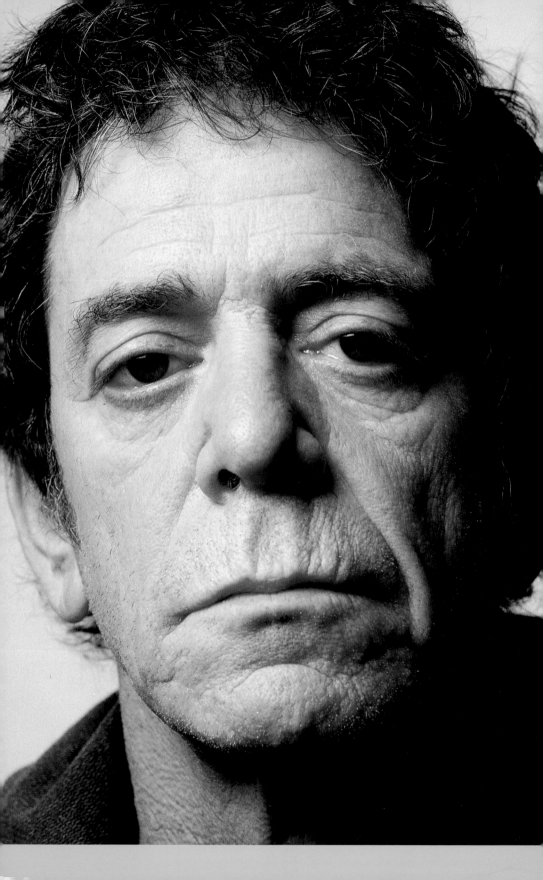

"A German group called Zeitkratzer gets in touch with me, they're a ten-piece orchestra. They get in touch with me. 'Can we play *Metal Machine Music* live?' I said, 'It's impossible. It can't be done.' They said, 'Let us try. We transcribed it. Let us send you a few minutes of it and you tell us.' They sent me it and I played it and there it was! It was unbelievable! I said, 'My God! Okay, go do it.' They said, 'Will you play guitar on the fourth part of it?' And I said, 'That would be awesome, to do that guitar live.' So *Metal Machine Music* finally got performed live at the Berlin Opera House. I have videotapes of the whole thing. It's extraordinary that you can do something like that because all those years ago it was considered a career ender. And it almost was, believe you me!" 2003

"I put out *Metal Machine Music* to clear the air and get rid of all those fucking assholes who show up at the show and yell 'Vicious' and 'Walk On Yhe Wild Side'." 1977

"There were rumours that I couldn't stand tours because I was on dope and my mind was going. I put out *Metal Machine Music* precisely to put a stop to all of it. It wasn't ill advised at all. It did what it was supposed to do." 1977

"It was all so boring. Then along came *Metal Machine Music*. It was like a bomb. The idea was good in itself but for the full impact you had to go through all the motions of execution." 1977

"It was after *Berlin* and *Rock 'N' Roll Animal*. They thought, 'A-ha more!' and they got it and it was 'ARGGHHH' what is this? A double album of what? They should have been given a chance to have their say about it. They were supposed to have something that let them know. So people heard it and were like, 'Are you crazy?' RCA said that after *Metal Machine Music* they were never going to let me make another record in my life. Then they kindly said, 'We'll let you make another record if you swear that it will be NOTHING like *Metal Machine Music*.'" 2000

SOLO IN THE SEVENTIES

"When I was in Japan they liked it. There are about seven thousand different melodies going on at one time or another and each time around there's more: like harmonics increase and melodies increase, in a different combination again. I don't expect anybody with no musical background to get it. I took classical piano for fifteen fucking years, theory, composition, the whole thing, and I'm getting so fucking tired of people saying, 'Oh it's a rock'n'roll guy fucking around with electronic music'. That's bullshit. One of these days I'm gonna pull my degreees out and say, 'Does that make me legitimate'. But I don't wanna' do that because that's horseshit too. So Neil Sedaka went to Juillard, so what else is new? But like I told some of the ad people at RCA, they said it's freaky. I said right, and Stravinsky's 'Firebird' is freaky.**"** 1976

"There's some frequencies on there that are dangerous. What I'm talking about is like in France they have a sound gun. It's a weapon. It puts out frequencies which kill people, just like they do operations with sound. It's a very delicate brain operation, they have surgical instruments that are sound. They've had this weapon since 1945. Hitler didn't have it, the French did of all people. Maybe that's why they play such bad rock n roll." 1976

"I'm not gonna apologise to anybody for *Metal Machine Music* and I don't think any disclaimer should've been put on the cover. Just because some kid paid $7.98 for it, I don't care if they pay $59.98 or $75 for it, they should be grateful I put that fucking thing out and if they don't like it they can go eat ratshit. I make records for me." 1976

Coney Island Baby (1975)

"They're not what people think of as archetypcal Lou Reed songs but they forgot like on the first Velvets album,' I'll Be Your Mirror', 'Femme Fatale'. I've always liked that kind of stuff and now you're going to have a whole album full of it. *The Many Moods Of Lou Reed,* just like Johnny Mathis and if they don't like it they can shove it. It's the kinda stuff you'd play if you were in a bar and you didn't wanna hear about it. It's the Brooklyn-Long Island axis at work. Like you know the Harptones 'Glory of Love', doo wop, I wanted to rip that off them but not use the song, do my own." 1976

"They're great fucking songs." 1976

"All the albums I put out after this are going to be things I want to put out. No more bullshit, no more dyed hair, faggot junkie trip. I mimic me better than anyone else so if everybody else is making money ripping me off, I figure maybe I better get in on it. Why not? I created Lou Reed. I have nothing even faintly in common with that guy, but I can play him well, really well." 1976

Rock And Roll Heart (1976)

"There was just Rachel and me living at the Gramercy Park Hotel on $15 a day while the lawyers were trying to figure out what to do with me. Then I got a call from Clive Davis. I felt like saying, 'You mean you want to be seen with me in public?' I knew then I'd won." 1975

SOLO IN THE SEVENTIES

"I had a couple of songs before we went in the studio but they changed. The rest I wrote in the studio. It's much more fun that way. It isn't expensive because I'm very quick. It took twenty-seven days to record that album including mixing. It took as long to mix as it did to record. I just had the basic progressions, of two or three chords, but no lyrics." 1976

"Clive Davis wanted to sweeten it up, horns or strings or something. He argued that the title song had potential to really be radio-worthy if we just did that to it. I'm a control person. I fought so hard to get things to the point of having that control that I wouldn't relinquish it." 1976

"On other albums I let other people do what they liked, this time I got serious and played what I liked. Every track. There's lots of very dumb rock'n'roll songs on it but then I like dumb rock'n'roll. It's very hard to find a dumb guitar player and a dumb piano player, everyone's so much into being technically together. But I fit the bill, because I play very stupid." 1976

Street Hassle (1978)

"When Clive heard the original, which is 2' 11" long, he said that it was great and I should make it longer. So I did. 'Street Hassle' is basically a two minute odd tape loop. The basic track's all the same but with different overdubs put over it. It shows how many ways you can look at the same thing. What I did was record a whole string section but I only used part of it – the cello. I only brought in the whole string section for one part, so it kind of sweeps in real panoramic. I had three vignettes, so I thought the perfect thing here was to dissolve, like in a movie, shift one set of music past another set, sort of pan them and BOOM you're into the second world." 1978

"The Velvet Underground were banned from the radio. I'm still being banned. And for exactly the same reasons. Maybe they don't like Jewish faggots. No, it's what they think I stand for they don't like. They don't want their kid sitting around masturbating to some rock and roll record, probably one of mine. They don't want their kid ever to know he can snort coke or get a blow job at school or fuck his sister up the ass. They never have. But how seriously can you take it? So they won't play me on the radio. What's the radio? Who's the radio run by? Who's it played for? With or without the radio, I'm still dangerous to parents." 1978

"I was playing with a thing called Binaural Sound and I just had this long lyric and it seemed to divide itself up into three sections. So I was trying to put together three sections and then figure out how to go from section one to section two to section three. And there was this string part. The arranger was a great guy who said, You could probably do it better than anybody because you know this whole thing. And I said, Yeah but I can't write it out. And he said, You don't have to. All you have to do is hum it or sing it. So I did it. And then it was easy. I just took the string part apart and took the cellist or something who was playing a certain line and used that to go to another part. And that solved the problem. It was all just a mix. Then you could go from part one to part two to part three." 2000

SOLO IN THE SEVENTIES

"*Street Hassle* is the best album I've done. *Coney Island Baby* was a good one, but I was under siege. *Berlin* was *Berlin*, *Rock And Roll Heart* is good compared to the rest of the shit that's going around. As opposed to *Street Hassle*, they're all babies. If you wanna' make adult rock records, you gotta' take care of all the people along the way. And it's not child's play. You're talking about managers, accountants, you're talking about the lowest level of human beings. *Street Hassle* is me on the line. And I'm talking to them one to one." 1978

"There's a lot of songs people don't even notice that are my favorites, and they might come under the umbrella of stupid. Like 'Senselessly Cruel' and 'Shooting Star' – I love that orchestral guitar at the beginning. It's one of the greatest things I ever did, and no one – zero – has ever noticed it." 2000

"Bruce Springsteen was mixing in the studio below us and I thought, 'How fortuituous'. People expect me to badmouth him because he's from New Jersey but I think he's really fabulous. He did the part so well that I had to bury him in the mix. I knew Bruce would do that recitation seriously because he really is of the street, you know." 1978

BRUCE SPRINGSTEEN & WIFE PATTY SCIALFA

Take No Prisoners (1979)

“It's a comedy album. Lou Reed talks and talks and talks.**”** 1979

The Bells (1979)

“My expectations are very high, to be the greatest writer that ever lived on God's earth. In other words, I'm talking about Shakespeare, Dostoevsky. I want to do that rock and roll thing that's on a level with *The Brothers Karamazov*. I'm starting to build up a body of work. I'm on the right track.”

ON WRITING *THE BELLS*, 1979

“You know I love the title track. I love the lyric. It was ad-libbed on the spot which was fun to do. It was just one take. It's interesting to just come up with it, whatever it is, wherever it comes from.**”**

2000

“Most of the songs were co-written with the band which is something I hadn't done since the Velvets.” 1979

“I think that's a great sounding album. One of my favourites. The older I get, the more meaningful it becomes to me. No one liked it when it came out and nobody seems to have changed their mind about it since. I love it, though. You know, some of the best things I've ever done have barely been noticed. Or just dismissed out of hand. Even *Berlin* when it came out – totally dismissed. *Metal Machine Music* – everybody hated that.**”** **2004**

SOLO IN THE SEVENTIES

Lifestyle

On Sexuality

"You can't fake being gay. If they claim they're gay, they're going to have to make love in a gay style and most people aren't capable of making that commitment. That line everyone's bisexual – I think that's just meaningless." 1973

"I have such a heavy resentment thing because of all the prejudices against me being gay. How can anybody gay keep their sanity?"

1979

"I just wouldn't want my listeners to be under a false impression. I want them to know, if they're liking a man, that it's a gay one, from top to bottom." 1979

"You know a lot of women get very tired of being needed. They think, I want you to pick me up and throw me through the window and say, 'Ah fuck you'. I'm a chauvinist down to my toes. I think women admire force all the more for not having it. It's axiomatic that a woman is all the more impressed that you could kill her. A woman can get turned off if you're appreciative of her when what she really wants is to be smacked across the mouth. My attitude often tends to be, 'Screw you too and I'll screw your girlfriends just for spite'. Which is a terrible way to do things because it's not like I would enjoy it. Of course they would, it goes without saying." **1979**

"You wanna know the real Lou Reed? Turn round. Now bend over."

1979

On Drugs And Alcohol

"I drink constantly. It destroys the nervous system. I'm getting tired of liquor because there's just nothing strong enough." **1973**

"I still do shoot speed. My doctor gives it to me. Well no actually they're just shots of meth mixed with vitamins. Well no actually they're just Vitamin C injections." 1973

"Speed kills. I'm not a speed freak." **1975**

"I'm into drug masturbation." 1977

"I've never made any bones about the fact that I take amphetamines. Any sane person would every chance they get. But I'm not in favour of legalisation because I don't want all those idiots running around grinding their teeth at me. I only take Methedrine which most people don't realise is a vitamin. Vitamin M. If people don't realise how much fun it is listening to *Metal Machine Music*, let 'em smoke their fucking marijuana, which is just bad acid anyway, and we've already been through that and forgotten it. I don't make records for fucking flower children." **1976**

"I used to take acid. You discover the universal truth in about four hours, forget it in the fifth and in the sixth, you're hungry." 1978

"I don't take drugs. I want people to take drugs." **1974**

"In the late Seventies I started to search for the perfect sound, whatever that might be, before that I was mainly interested in drugs, insanity and the rock'n'roll lifestyle. I cleaned up my act because otherwise I would have kicked the bucket. So, I started to search for another insanity. I started chasing the perfect sound, the perfect album. It's just another way to survive." 1998

Enter Sylvia

❝She's nothing special, just a sexy little girl.❞ ANDY WARHOL, 1981

❝I now know that certain things will get taken care of and looked
out for on the home front where you can get hurt a lot. It's nice
to have a trustworthy situation at home, a security situation.
It's good to know that you're covered and beyond just friendship,
I'm a great one for commitment. I like to look at centuries passed
when knighthood was in flower – I'm still a great one for that.
I think I've found my flower so it makes me feel more like a
knight.❞ 1980

❝Lou was very reclusive, he doesn't like to be vulnerable at all.
He's very protective of himself and understandably, he's had a
rough life. When he married Sylvia, she became his barrier, and
when I was travelling with him in 1974, Rachel was his barrier.
He kept people between him, I remember calling Lou on the phone
when he was married to Sylvia and she got on the phone and was
'Who is this? What do you want?' She grilled me on why I was
calling and then finally she said, 'I don't know where he is' and she
hung up. Then he called me back five minutes later because he
realized I wasn't after him for anything, so he could talk to me and
called me back. He's a very frightened person in a lot of ways.❞

DOUG YULE, 1995

❝I really love it. It smells great. Even if you wanted to do
something, there's nothing here. It's appalling how much sleep
I get. I'm a happy person. And I would hope somebody like me
would be. You ought to be happy. I'm happy I'm walking around
alive. I'm happy about my personal situation. And from where
I look out.❞ ON BUYING A HOUSE IN RURAL NEW JERSEY, 1983

❝I'm glad my wife was there when I met President Havel, because
otherwise I'd just think I dreamed it.❞ 1993

LIFESTYLE

Cleaning Up

"I tried to give up drugs by drinking." 1993

"The man turned up many times. I was as bad as it gets. Then, at a certain point in the Eighties, I got married, joined AA and started playing more guitar." **2004**

"I believe in all things in moderation – including moderation. I did more than abuse my body in the past. I very often wounded it. I enjoy age. I was miserable when I was younger." 1979

"The last thing in the world I would be interested in is blowing it on a personal health level. I think drugs are the single most terrible thing and if I thought there was anything I could do which I thought might be effective in stopping people dealing in drugs and taking them, I would do it. I just think it's the worst conceivable thing in the world. Before, I didn't care. Speaking for myself, I could not continue that way. When drugs and liquor turn on you, it becomes debilitating rather than energising or making you more focused. Then it's just a terrible jumble. So I had to set about starting at square one again." **1981**

"There's this umbilical cord that goes between Lou Reed and I. Lou was on the same treatment (Inteferon drug treatment for liver damage). He was on tour when he did the treatment, which I can't imagine. I heard horror stories about that tour. I was lucky enough to be at home for three months working on other records. It gives you flu symptoms so what you do is take it with heavy duty aspirin every other night and Lou was also doing it every other night before he went to sleep and he was on tour."

JOHN CALE ON GETTING CLEAN, 1998

"I'm not interested in any morality plays. I'm not proselytising but as far as my early demise goes, I've made a lot of efforts in the other direction. Such things you might consider dull – working out, playing basketball, keeping my head together and all that. I find destructive people very, very boring and I'd like to think that I'm not one of them." **1983**

LIFESTYLE

Solo In The Eighties

THE ALBUMS

Growing Up In Public (1980)

❝*Growing Up In Public* has some great lyrics like 'My Old Man' which I always thought had a great lyric. And the lead song was pretty good, including the title.❞ 2000

❝A composite picture of a certain kind of personality, not necessarily mine.❞ 1980

❝For the last few years I was working with musicians who were into jazz and funk. I wasn't playing guitar on my records because I really couldn't play with those guys, being a simple rock and roll player. I thought it would be interesting to explore that direction but there was a gap between me and them. You can hear it on the records. So I said, 'You've carried this experiment far enough. It's not working. The ideas are there and then they disappear, the music isn't consistent, you seem isolated, there's a certain confidence that's not there because you're not really in control.' So I dissolved the band.❞ 1982

The Blue Mask (1982)

❝There was a big time span between *Growing Up In Public* and *The Blue Mask*. A lot of changes took place. I had a completely new band, a new batch of people and some time to think about where you go from here. *The Blue Mask* sounds great. I started really wanting to do it better. We got a good sound out of that studio which was the size of a football field. We played really, really loud there. When you were playing, you could barely hear another person.❞ 2000

❝Musically, the first week and a half was really great, out of the four years. We did *The Blue Mask*. It's a record that I'm really proud of. There was no rehearsing, no overdubs, no punch-ins for mistakes. The exact opposite of The Voidoids. I inspired and encouraged him to play guitar again. I didn't have a lot of fun with him but at least it's out there and I'm proud of that. With that record, Fernando Saunders and Duane Perry were taken aback by this primitive playing. There was an intensity there and we reacted to each

WITH DAVE STEWART

other as musicians. It isn't a jazz record but there's that kind of sensitivity. He listened to some wild ideas I brought in like with 'Waves Of Fear' - he had nothing to lose at that point as he'd just done *Growing Up In Public*. It's just a shame - I'd still be with him now and put up with whatever personal problems I had with him. But he's not a nice guy. In one way, he respected me. If he yelled at me, I'd yell back. I'm outspoken and don't take crap from people. His problem is that he likes to be surrounded by yes men that flatter him but he's smart enough to know what's going on and he hates them for it and he ends up with a lot of hack musicians.❞ ROBERT QUINE, 1997

SOLO IN THE EIGHTIES ❞

"My best album to date. This one was pretty much perfect. It came out the way it was supposed to." 1982

"*The Blue Mask* was a very big critical success but it didn't sell well. It built up his confidence though. By the time we did *Legendary Hearts* in late '82, he was much more of a control freak. He was rejecting ideas that I brought in. He was feeling pretty precious about his career. His biggest weakness is that he wants to be regarded as a poet. The more conscious he is of this, the worse songs he writes. It could have been a pretty good record. It wasn't going to be as good as the last one: the songs weren't as good. The atmosphere was really uptight.
It's impossible to be friends with him. When I got the final mix, I was really freaked out. He pretty much mixed me off the record. I was in Ohio and took it out in the driveway and smashed the tape into pieces. I didn't talk to him for a month but he knew what he'd done. I have cassettes of the rough mix of the record and it was a really good record but he made it all muddy and murky." ROBERT QUINE 1997

"My goal has always been to make an album that would speak to people the way Shakespeare speaks to me, the way Joyce speaks to me, something with that kind of power, something with bite to it." 1982

"I'm very very image conscious and I've tried to use it gracefully, to focus it. On this album I'm bringing all those Lou Reeds together, into one. But the basic image is and always has been Lou Reed comes from New York City and writes rock and roll songs."

1982

“About a week before going in the studio I got together with the guitar player and we ran down the songs together. I wrote it all out beforehand. Everyone knew the songs up to a point, but nothing was too structured.”

1982

“Here are two people engaged in violent behaviour towards one another and it's an attempt at salvation that they know can't occur and a redemption that doesn't exist. It's too much for them, they're past that, they're torturing each other, they're wearing dark blue masks.” ON THE TITLE TRACK, 1982

“I have found without exception that any guy who listens to 'The Gun' reacts with universal fear. And it's dangerous for me too. If I do a song and there's a bad character or a drug character or something like that – sometimes it's me and sometimes it's not me – as I sing the song, I go through it. It's a really cathartic kind of thing in a lot of ways. It is acting. But doing these characters long enough, it gets you. Some of those lyrics are very rough.” 1982

WITH ELVIS COSTELLO

“I'm not going to tour anymore, period. It wasn't good for me. I wasn't happy with my band. Still, I did have fun. Now I could possibly see playing New York, maybe one night at the Bottom Line. But as for 90 days and 89 cities, I can't do that anymore. I used to drink a lot. And it would be hard for me to imagine getting through one of those tours without slipping back. And I don't want to do that.” 1982

SOLO IN THE EIGHTIES ”

Legendary Hearts (1983)

❝I've always liked those very basic very simple rock and roll changes. I've never heard anything I like more than that. Not in opera, not in classical music, not in jazz nor in show tunes. Not movie music. Nothing. Nothing has impresesed me as much as the most basic rock and roll chord change and by that I mean E to A. And to this day when I hear that change done right – and it can

be done wrong - I get an abnormal degree of pleasure from it. Wouldn't it be wonderful to put a melody over that, something that would stick like grease? And then wouldn't it be great if the lyrics also had some substance to them, were as simple and as elegant as that change from one chord to the other?❞ 1983

❝'The Last Shot' – that was a monstrous song. My God, wouldn't want to listen to that one now. But it was so great. It's the perfect rock song. I mean, it does it all. That one stays with you. Did I write it to deal with drink cravings? No no no no no. That's not what I wrote it. I wrote it because I believed it. Because I'd thought it so many times. I mean, you know, kind of officially wishing it was your last shot. You know, like, this is the last drink. This one. Right here. OK. Everybody. Listen. I'm going to really enjoy this one. And then, that's it! And of course, nothing remotely like that happens. But you wish it did. It was just this fantasy. It was absurd. I mean, if you really think about it, you're talking about life and death stuff, that's not going to happen. It probably helped people? I didn't write it to help anybody. Not even myself? No, not even me. I mean, maybe it did. But I just write to write. I don't completely understand it. I can say I do, but I don't.❞ 2000

Live In Italy (1983)

"We did some more touring. He just happened to record bad concerts like *Live In Italy*. The band was sensitive enough that we were capable of improvising like on 'Sister Ray' and 'Heroin' which we only did once. He had to teach it to the others but I knew it already. But there was more and more of a strain between us. About a day before *New Sensations* was going to be recorded, he fired me and did the guitar himself. I did do the tour with him afterwards, that was a long tour. I came to him and said, 'Forget whatever happened, I just want to play with you'. By this time, we had an awful band. The new drummer would only play well in rehearsals and the keyboard player (Peter Woods) worked with Al Stewart and Cyndi Lauper. There wasn't much room to improvise. At the end of 'Kill Your Sons', I'd do a drone and Lou would do a guitar solo, we'd get pretty far out there. This keyboard player thought it was joke and play with his feet - Lou would have to come over and tell him to stop. Because I wasn't on *New Sensations*, I didn't have a lot to add live. I'd be doing a song, playing D and G for six minutes like 'Doing The Things That We Want To' which I didn't really like, with no variation and the keyboard guy playing accordian. I thought, 'This is not why I got a guitar and wanted to play in a rock and roll band.' We hated each other's guts, me and the keyboard player. Lou got really abusive at the end – he'd hog all the guitar solos and made sure I got mixed out – even live. I got back from the tour and decided that was it. I assumed he knew it. He'd put me down to the rest of the band, knowing that they'd tell me about it later.**"** ROBERT QUINE 1997

New Sensations (1984)

"I think it's different sounding to *The Blue Mask* and *Legendary Hearts* because I'm the only guitar player on it. 'New Sensations', the title track, is a phenomenal song even though I hate the synth on it. I like 'I Love You Suzanne' and 'Doin' The Things We Want to'. I don't like the background voices on that song though. I can't stand them." 2000

SOLO IN THE EIGHTIES

Mistrial (1986)

"I think the album is a very up album. I think somebody in my situation should be positive. At this stage of the game it would be, possibly, disappointing to other people as well as to myself had it not been a positive album. I mean after all, I'm getting paid to do something I want to do anyway. I don't have to work for a living. I don't have to go through a whole bunch of things I couldn't bear. I just think I'm very lucky and that attitude is reflected on the record I think. I want everyone watching to forget everything else and just listen to the music and to have lots of positive energy and emotional moments. I think this is all any singer can hope for."

1986

"It's got 'Tell It To Your Heart' and 'Video Violence', but I don't think it's as well recorded as it could have been. I don't like the production. I had a lot of trouble with the producer on that. We were battling constantly and it made life difficult. We were pushing in opposite directions. If someone doesn't get it, they're not going to either. That's one of the things I've learned over the years: if they don't get it, stop there, it's not going to get better. They're not going to suddenly turn around and say, 'Oh I get it'. He just didn't get it and you just get antagonistic when people don't get it. There were a lot of ugly fights going on." 2000

New York (1989)

"I can't do anything outside of New York. It's death." 1974

"What *New York* is about, over and above what I'm singing about is the use of language." 1989

"I think of myself as a writer, working through rock and roll as a medium and doing it from here, New York." 1998

"This is my vision of what a rock and roll album can be. Put it this way. I'm writing for an educated or self-educated person who has reached a certain level. I'm not aiming *New York* at fourteen year olds." 1989

"Supposedly when you get older, you get something from all of it before or you drop dead and that's the end of it. I think I know about certain things better than other people.**"** 1989

"They kept saying, 'Don't you have anything you left off? Why should somebody buy the single if they've already got the album?' I said when they put *Moby Dick* out do you think they said, 'In the paperback version let's leave out chapter thirteen?' Anyway I didn't have anything. Then I said, 'I remember one little jam Mike and I did that was great fun. Maybe I can find it on cassette.'"

ON THE B-SIDE TO DIRTY BLVD, 1989

SOLO IN THE EIGHTIES "

Politics & Advertising: The New Lou

The Honda Ads (1985)

66 Who else could make a scooter hip? 99 1986

66 Reed is an innovator, one of the pioneers of new music. His music is unique and experimental – much like scooters. 99

NEIL LEVENTHAL, MOTOR SCOOTER
MANAGER, HONDA, 1985

American Express Ads (1985)

66 How to buy a jacket. 99 THE TAGLINE ON AMERICAN EXPRESS ADS DEPICTING
LOU REED IN TRADEMARK LEATHER JACKET, 1985

LOU REED *Talking*

Farm Aid (1985)

"I'd show up out there (his house in rural New Jersey) and go, What the fuck is going on? It's raining here. What is this, another weekend with rain? Finally they sat me down to tell me the facts of life such as there are farmers out there and they're getting killed by the drought. I became aware of what the weather means besides New Yorkers going away for the weekend.**"** 1987

Sun City/Artists Against Apartheid (1985)

"I couldn't not be vocal about apartheid.**"** 1987

The Amnesty International Tour (1986)

"I had never been a member of a group besides a rock band but I've joined Amnesty International. In a country where Reagan is President, it is very easy to be cynical. But I'm really fascinated about why people are arrested and what happens to them in jail. I mean, for the rock and roll records I've made, I'd be dead ten times over if I was over there.**"** 1986

Back With John Cale: Songs For Drella 1998/1990

"Lou came to a performance of The Falklands Suite after Andy died. We then got together over a period of three weeks around Christmas 1988 in a rehearsal room up on Ninth Avenue and 50th Street. I came up with the concept of *Songs For Drella* and then went to Harvey Lichtenstein, head of the Brooklyn Academy of Music, and arranged for us to perform it there. We had our texts, we sat down, the tapes were running. I've still got all the tapes and they're really interesting to listen to. You can hear how the *Songs For Drella* were written as we sat around and reminisced extensively about Andy. Lou told me things I didn't know."

JOHN CALE, 1999

"The immediate difference was that there was a schedule. We had three weeks to finish it. Ten days to write it, two weeks to rehearse. We had all the opportunities in the world. We just wanted to do something about Andy. We had some musical lawyers arrange some dates and we figured out a three week period. It was all planned. I still have all the tapes of every session – so does he - how we got to the arrangements, how ideas were formed, things we broke down, phrases we re-arranged." JOHN CALE, 1998

LOU REED *Talking*

"After I'd written all the music and we'd got all the song structures together, Lou went off and wrote all the lyrics, which were immaculate." **JOHN CALE, 1999**

"We began recording immediately after the second performance at the Brooklyn Academy of Music in 1989. Confronting each other every day got worse and worse. In the studio, Lou would smoke and blow it in my face, knowing full well that I hated it. He and his guitar player Mike Rathke ganged up, as if they were trying to push me off the record." JOHN CALE, 1999

"John and I just rented out a small rehearsal studio for three weeks and locked ourselves in. I was really excited by the amount of power just two people could do without needing drums because what we have there is such a strong core idea that the simpler the better." **1988**

The Velvet Underground Reunion

Cartier Foundation (1990)

"The Cartier Foundation approached Sylvia Reed with the idea of a reunion of the Velvets, inviting Lou and me to play at the opening of its Andy Warhol Exposition outside Paris on 15 June, 1990. The event also included a multimedia homage to the Velvet Underground." JOHN CALE, 1999

"We kicked into 'Heroin', which we hadn't played in twenty-two years and it was just the same as always. As I got off stage after playing 'Heroin' I was at the point of tears." JOHN CALE, 1998

"There were no roadies, we humped our own gear. And the video footage is like watching four guys pottering around the back yard on a Saturday afternoon, tuning up. Then, all of a sudden, it kicked in, as if we'd finally taken the shackles off. It was very powerful. All the gang from the old days were there too and after we had played, it was as if we were inseparable – Andy's gang again. Fifteen of us would go places together. It was really nostalgic and sad in a way." JOHN CALE, 1999

LOU REED *Talking*

The Reunion Tour, (1993)

❝Great fun, for a month.**❞** 1995

❝Nothing would have got done without Lou thinking it was a good idea. There was nothing scheduled for him for 1993 so he decided to try it.❞ JOHN CALE, 1999

❝The most sadness I had about it falling apart was that it was so nice to have everybody together, being friends again. To see that get blown away, that made me very sad 'cause we had such a good time on that tour. We had not been together, the four of us in one place, in YEARS. I was real happy about that. It was really

disappointing to have the fighting start again. But we didn't do that tour thinking that we were going to restart the Velvets. That wasn't the idea at all. For me, it was just 'Oh boy, is this going to be fun!' Especially in Europe, those are the people who have supported us for all these years and we hadn't played there ever. It was great to go there and play for these people who had been paying my rent. I thought it was going to be great because I knew that they'd be thrilled to death. So, that was my thing. That's what I wanted to do - I can't speak for the others though. It was like a thank you.**❞**

MO TUCKER, 1998

❝We all agreed from the get-go that we were not going to parody ourselves – as Lou had for twenty years.❞ JOHN CALE, 1999

" One night in Bologna I was doing 'Waiting For The Man' with a huge orchestral introduction and I was trying to give them the tempo from the piano but I was too far away. Lou went and told my tech to turn the piano off. At that point I was ready to knock his teeth down his throat. **"** JOHN CALE, 1998

" Lou pretty effectively killed things. He did what he wanted to. The worst part of all was that Sterling was getting sick at the same time as these problems with Lou. When you really put a lot of faith in somebody and then you're let down time after time after time then you still have a real problem just walking away because you've invested so much emotional energy into this situation. And you've seen it develop and grow and you've been kind of rewarded that it's very difficult to say that's it, it's not going to work anymore. And that's what I had to do with Lou. It was the way he spoke to Mo Tucker that really did it. I just thought, the guy's out of control, I'm not going to try any more. **"**

JOHN CALE, 1998

THE VELVET UNDERGROUND REUNION

Laurie Anderson

"Laurie is like the sun.**"** 2003

"Lou's a sweet person. He has a very good relationship with Laurie Anderson which he's had for twelve, fifteen years. I know from two women I spoke to – his first wife and a long-time girlfriend who he was with for ten years from his college years onwards, that he is very sweet when you get closely involved with him romantically."

VICTOR BOCKRIS, 2005

"Well, I think he's probably made me a little tougher. And by that I mean if I'm sort of talking around something, he just goes, 'Why don't you just say what you really think? OK? You don't have to be nice or pretend.' So that's been very interesting. And maybe it's almost the opposite thing that he's learning from me. You know, I'm kind of like, 'You don't really have to say that straight out. You can maybe take another turn around before you do it.' But of course the best thing is that I never know what to expect from Lou. It's great to be with someone who's always surprising you with his opinions and thoughts. That's very exciting. **" LAURIE ON LOU, 1996**

**" My partner Laurie Anderson told me I could draw. Because I've always admired Robert Crumb, he's a terrific draftsman when he wants to be. Laurie is too. She said, 'You can draw, draw an airplane.' So I drew this pathetic airplane. And she said, 'There you go! Now just practice it.' Believe me, when they say, 'He can't draw a straight line', they're talking about me. I'm made for computer art where you can disguise all of that." ** 2002

" I do try to make things simpler, and more to the point. Lou is very encouraging to me in this. If I'm hiding behind a simile, he'll say 'Why don't you just say what you mean, instead of alluding to things all the time?' And sometimes he's really right. **"**

LAURIE ANDERSON, 2005

LAURIE ANDERSON

The Books

Between Thought And Expression (1993)

66 Well, I've always had the view that the lyric should be able to stand alone before it gets married to music. I just got a list of all the songs and picked out the ones I thought stood alone the best. If I even had a question about it I just took it out. The other thing was whether it contributed to a narrative form. There's a narrative link that takes you through three decades, so they follow each other and make sense. Certain themes became really apparent that you might otherwise not be so aware of. 99 1993

Pass Thru Fire: The Collected Lyrics (2000)

66 I have always thought my lyrics went beyond reportage and took emotional albeit nonmoral stances. 99 **2000**

Emotion In Action (2002)

66 I live on intuition and taking pictures is intuitive. 99 2002

66 Photography is visual music. 99 **2005**

Solo In The Nineties

THE ALBUMS

Magic And Loss (1992)

❝There are novels and there are plays and this is at least the equal of those – maybe a bit more.❞ 1992

❝It's my dream album, because everything finally came together to where the album is finally fully realised. I got it to do what I wanted it to do, commercial thoughts never entered into it, so I'm just stunned.❞ **1993**

❝I think on *Magic And Loss* eventually you have to take a swing at the major themes and certainly loss and death is one of them.❞

1993

LOU REED *Talking* ❞

❝I remember Seymour Stein (head of Sire) saying, 'Woa is this about cancer?' It was about losing friends to an illness. Magic, the magic of life and loss. That's what it's about, that album. First, I was interested in writing an album about magic because some friends of mine had told me about real magicians in Mexico. So I thought, 'I wanna see something like that. I want to write an album about magic and maybe somebody will get in touch with me and show me something'. And then tragedy struck and I hadn't really experienced that before and there was nothing to listen to that would cheer me up. And I realised that there was nothing I knew of that covered that experience. And it just wrote itself and that was it. And I thought, 'Maybe this one you should keep to yourself'. You know, Fine you got it out of your system, you wrote it, now put it away. No one wants to hear this. Go on to something else. But it was, NO WAY. I was possessed. I mean, oh my god, I get very difficult and possessed sometimes. Then I went on tour and insisted on playing the album from beginning to end which was not what a lot of people in the audience wanted. I remember the record company guys going, 'What do you want to do that for? Then they know what the next number is, there's no surprise'. And I said, 'There's no surprise in Beethoven's Fifth'. I mean, what is this? I thought it was a really special thing, well, it was to me. I don't know if people got it. People seem to come to that album later, and it's always for the same reason. Something happened. Some of the records, the more life experience you have, the more they make sense. And if you haven't, then it doesn't. People who like that record are people who have been visited by the real world. I suppose there's classical music like a mass or something but this is different. There's a physical voice to it and it's not in Latin. But you know, I was glad they even put it out. Back to Seymour, I said, 'Do you not want to put it our or something?' And he said, 'No no it's a really important album.' So I said, 'Here it is.'**❞** 2000

❝It may be out of print by now, for all I know. It didn't do very well. You could say, Why would you think it would? You have to really listen to that one.❞ 2000

"With Doc Pomus (one friend for whom Lou wrote *Magic And Loss*) they left his answering machine on for a long time because everybody loved to call up and hear his voice on it. He was such a remarkable guy. That's where that line came from. I lost two people in one year. We're strong willed but we're fragile. Things happen to us. That's a fact." 2000

"What would happened if I hadn't written *Magic And Loss*? That's a hypothesis. That's not what happened. I try not to deal with what ifs? It's hard enough dealing with just what's there. I'm sure writing something made me feel better, that it transformed things into something. It certainly doesn't make you feel worse. Yeah, writing things makes you feel better. Writing about everything makes you feel better. Writing about everything makes me feel better, just not at the time I'm writing it. Later. With any kind of luck." 2000

"I did the best I could with it, it's not something I would like to do again. And I certainly don't intend to but then, on the other hand, I didn't intend to do that one. It was a surprise. But once I started writing it, I couldn't stop." 2000

Set The Twilight Reeling (1996)

"The song 'Set The Twilight Reeling' is about growing and changing, getting better. It's just change. I just am always in flux. Put it that way. It does get interesting to find out who and what you are." 1995

"'Trade In' - that's a great song. Once in a while I get a song like that and no one notices it. I love the lyrics to it, everything. I thought it really captured that certain kind of 'oh you sweet thing'." 2000

> **"I produced this. And I wanted you to hear what I heard. That's the idea. You're only virgin once. The first time you hear a record that's the way you hear it. This is the thing I've been trying to get for a long time. This CD sounds exactly right."**
>
> 1995

Perfect Night Live (1998)

> **"**It's a live album and that means something new, a new beginning. It was a perfect night, a magic night and I don't really want to talk about that night because it's very intimate. I don't think there will be another perfect night in my life.**"** 1998

> **"It was THE perfect night, everything was right and I wanted to have a document, a memory of the night. I'm a musician, so, of course, it's an album. I believe it's a great album, an album everybody should have. It's authentic and not a lot of rock'n'roll records are really authentic. I don't like overdubs, never liked them. I don't want to change reality, but I felt that the night we recorded it was magic. It's simple but that's just it. It doesn't need anything else."** 1998

> **"**Some even claim that I'm a terror, a dictator and they're right. But I'm also talented and I know when I created something great and *Perfect Night* is something great, no doubt, no buts. I'm too old to do things by half. I'm in this business for too long to be halfhearted about anything. When I record an album I'm trying to get as close as possible to that perfect moment. I try to capture as much of the magic as possible. *Perfect Night* has that magic and it has the raw energy that grabs you by the throat. That's how rock'n'roll should be. It has to be, to be real and honest.**"** 1998

> **"People say: 'It's not as electric as *Rock'n'Roll Animal*. Well, of course it's not. It's not supposed to be. I can't remake *Rock'n'Roll Animal*. I understand the impulse, though, I always wish Clint Eastwood would make another *Dirty Harry*."** 2004

On Songwriting

"Coming up with the idea. That's not the bitch. Unless you can't do it. Everything else is the bitch." **2003**

"I write about what I know." 2000

"One of my strong points is that I'm good at dialogue. I can make it sound like something someone said. A lot of my stuff sounds like the way people speak, when in fact it's not. It's sort of a polished version of the way people speak." **1984**

"I'm always studying people that I know and when I think I've got them worked, then I go away and write a song about them. When I sing that song, I become them. It's for that reason that I'm kind of empty when I'm not doing anything. I don't have a personality of my own, I just pick up on other people's." 1975

"You take the lyric and you push it forward so that it speaks to you on a personal level and still keeps the beat because I'm not talking about poetry reading. You can even make it dialogue between men and women. That could keep you occupied for the rest of your life." **1979**

"I keep a notebook. I also write in my head a lot or sometimes I'll write things out. It's much less a matter of doing the music first. Sometimes when that happens, it comes out of a riff. And what's a good riff? Sometimes you'll get locked into one and in the end you don't come out with a good song, just a riff." 1982

❝I write so everybody can understand. I'm a democrat.❞ 2005

❝There are certain kinds of songs you write that are just fun songs, the lyric really can't survive without the music. But for most of what I do, the idea behind it was to try and bring a novelist's eye to it, and, within the framework of rock and roll, to try to have that lyric there so somebody who enjoys being engaged on that level could have that and have the rock and roll too. Sometimes songs take years to get right. You do it and you just know it's not right and you can't get it right so you leave it. I think you can only do your best with it and sometimes your best isn't good enough. At which point you have to give it a rest. Because then you start doing really strange things to it. And when it starts going that far astray it's time to go away from it.❞ 1993

❝I used to have a notebook where I put stuff down. I stopped. Enough is enough already. I'm tired of hearing it. I'm doing other things. It's like a permanent radio station into my subconscious.❞

2002

❝Rock, that's what I get off on. I think there's real advantages to it: It's really fun, visceral, you really feel it. I love the idea of that power trying to explode through the speakers. I don't think of the records as passive. You bring them home and they can fuck with you. I like bringing it to life with the musicians. I get the kick out of doing that. I mean, I'm a musician, I like to play with the guys.❞ 1995

❝You can do serious things with it, you can talk about serious subjects in it. But it doesn't mean it loses its fun. It's pretty malleable. Even within that three-chord structure, there are so many things that can be done. And almost anybody can play guitar and almost everybody does. Words and music together can be so much more than the sum of their parts. It's that old thing - you put two things together and they make a third.❞ 1995

ON SONGWRITING

LOU REED *Talking*

"Later on I find out what the lyric to a song was really about. Lots of times I'll think it's about one thing and as I get a little distance from it - and by distance I mean like, say, seven or eight years – it suddenly becomes very obvious to me it was about something else entirely. It happens especially on stage. Periodically I do something older and I suddenly realise 'God listen to what this is about. I can't believe that I said this in public.' Some of the lyrics are really incredibly personal, and pretty accurate, so obviously so that it's always kind of funny, over the years, people continuously asking me, 'Are these things based on reality?' I thought it was so obvious that they were." 1993

"Sometimes I have the guitar riff, other times I've got the lyric first. There's no set rule for me. I take it wherever I can get it, however I can get it. That's fine. That's not the thing that I pay attention to. If I can come up with a title, if I have the title then I stuff that back here in my head and it'll take care of itself. I usually work out with Mike Rathke or Fernando. I've got a home studio, so I play around there first. What does this sound like? What do you think of this? I mean, I'm always calling Mike, Mike what do you think of this? Is it OK? What do you think? He's like, It's great, let's go play it. So he's like a good steadying influence so that I don't get caught up in going, Hmmm. So when he wants to play, I think, So let's just play it. See what it sounds like with two guitars. Let's see what happens." 2000

"You pay a price for that. Hey Lou, are you this? Are you that?"
ON WRITING CANDIDLY, 2000

"If you had a desire to learn to play, you sure could up to a point. You could certainly learn three chords and do a pop song. It's a great democracy. But at a certain point, desire won't get you there." 2002

"I wanted to combine Burroughs and Ginsberg with rock. I mean, here was this great music with not much going on lyrically, and here's a book like *Last Exit To Brooklyn*. You'd have to be retarded not to see the possibilities. I'm amazed that I pretty much still have the field to myself." 2003

ON WORKING WITH ROBERT WILSON

Timerocker (1996)

66We were interested in transcending time, passing through it and its various boundaries and worlds.99 2000

POEtry (2001)

66I saw it as a can't win situation.
I knew people would say 'How dare he rewrite Poe?' But I thought, here's the opportunity of a lifetime for real fun, to combine the kind of lyricism that he has into a flexible rock format. I really like my version of it. It's accessible, among other things. And I felt I was in league with the master. In that kind of psychology, that interest in the drives and the meaning of obsession and compulsion, in that realm Poe reigns supreme.99 2001

66I realized that when I was younger, I had really missed out on Poe - the subtleties, the nuances, the psychology. You can't just say he was macabre and had a sense of dread. He was interested in psychology - why you do things.99 2001

On Dealing With The Media

"Journalists mean nothing." 1977

" Most journalists would really like to come off looking a lot better than the subject. People lie. You have a journalist saying, 'Oh, my brother died of Aids, I'm so upset, do you know anyone who has had that?' And they are lying. There's no level too low. **"** 2005

"He's just a big schlub from Detroit. He's fat and he's got a moustache. I wouldn't shit in Lester's nose." ON LESTER BANGS, 1974

" I don't know anyone actually who does care what a critic says. **"**
2003

"Now photographers, most of them are Nazis. 'Move over there, tilt your head, do this, do that'. I said to a photographer once, 'Why do you do this?' He said, 'I love ordering people around. This is the only chance I get.' Not every journalist is like that, not every photographer either. But if you cue into the fact that odds are they are not on your side, then you play the game from your half of the net." 2005

LOU REED *Talking*

LOU REED *Talking*

On Acting

❝It's fun acting. I originally wanted to act. But I wasn't good enough. It's fun playing another character. I do that in songs all the time. Be a different age, wear different clothes. I used to sit around with my college room-mate and we would do *Waiting For Godot*. It was really good fun.❞ 2000

❝***Blue In The Face* is all improvised and I'm pretty funny, so it's just me and Paul and the sound guy. And Paul would ask me these questions and I would just rip and they'd edit it down to the funniest answers.**❞ 2000

❝Paul Auster thinks of me as his lucky mascot or something since *Blue In The Face*, so he wanted me to play this cameo role in *Lulu On The Bridge*.❞ 2000

Tai' Chi

"I found tai chi when I was studying with Leung Shum, who teaches Eagle Claw and Wu Hao (tai chi). And I'd been studying tai chi with him for a long time. In NY. Starting in the Eighties. There was a little break for world tours. And then I'd come back and I'd take up studying again. I had started also studying because I wanted to learn more about power and fighting. So I was studying how to generate power. And a lot of sparring with another great teacher Sifu Larry Tan, the founder of a Thai based system called Strange Dazzling Hands. And then, in

WITH ACTOR, JIMMY FALLON

my Wu class, one of my fellow students mentioned Ren to me. He said, 'You have got to see Master Ren'. And brought me a tape of him. And I saw the tape and then a friend of a friend's was in his class. And when I saw what they were doing, I said well, I've never seen tai chi that looked like this before and I wanted to learn it particularly as Master Shum was no longer teaching. But at first I didn't go because my friend said the class is so hard, it's impossible, it's really, really hard! But finally it was just too fascinating, so I went to the class and I met him and then I called around to see if I could study with him privately. When I saw what he did, I said oh my god, a man who can fly. I want to start learning that. And that was almost a year ago." 2003

LOU REED *Talking*

"My attitude is that you very rarely come in contact with someone of Master Ren's level, so every opportunity I could get to learn from him I wanted to do that. So I took time off from what I normally do. And I decided I really felt I was missing a lot of things in my tai chi education and that the answer to it was Master Ren. To show me the things that I hadn't been able to learn in some of the other classes. He combines the very beautiful form, the great control, the focus, and a really, truly remarkable power. When I saw that combination of grace and power, the fast and the soft, the yin and the yang, that's what I'd been looking for. When I started studying with him I realized how much he could teach me. To say the least. So I was very fortunate that he agreed to teach me. And I try to study with him as often as possible." **2003**

"From the minute I saw Master Ren do fajing, I thought I will study this forever. To try and get some of what he can do. And he's a truly great teacher. He likes showing you." 2003

"I try to do three hours of tai chi a day. It is a far more powerful force than any drug. It makes your dick really big!" **2004**

"I practise when I'm on tour. In the hotel I find out is there a conference room, a board room, and at some point there's bound to be one that's empty. In you go and you just lock it." 2003

"Well, everybody does something, some people race cars, others collect stamps, I find tai chi to be philosophically, aesthetically, physically and spiritually fascinating. I was told in my fast form there are four emotions you express. I found that a fascinating concept to have." **2003**

"Oh, you know, everything. Everything positive you could think of in every way. Mind, body, spirit, endurance, health, focus, discipline, physical strength. I'm talking about Chen Tai Chi specifically. The Tai Chi's you've probably seen are very slow but Chen Tai Chi is not slow." 2005

Solo In The Noughties

THE ALBUMS

Ecstasy (2000)

WITH WYCLEF JEAN

"This is not *New York* by any stretch of the imagination although people keep saying that it reminds them of *New York*. It doesn't remind me of it, not even a dot. As far as the guitar sounds, well yeah. But in everything to do with *Ecstasy*, the bar got raised a whole lot. There's still two guitars, bass, drums and some cellos and some horns but recorded a whole lot better. The sounds are better and more controlled in a certain way and I can play them better. I know what I'm doing more than on *New York*. Everything came together on this one. The focus is really good. There's a lot of words on this one. I like to think that I very slowly get better. Little incremental things get better and you add up these increments and pound for pound, this album weighs in pretty good." 2000

"I love you, I don't love you. You do love me but you don't love me enough. Or you love me but you won't marry me. Or vice versa. Real life. You've can't always have your way, whatever that is. When you're dealing with real people in life, it's complicated. The songs try to capture that odd push and pull that's going on, that can sometimes push you into a more extreme position than you would have realised. And you've gone and opened your mouth and you're stuck over there. And trying to have a balance with these things when you're dealing with emotion, that's difficult." 2000

"I was just told that the Greek root for ecstasy means 'standing outside yourself'. Everything's a story. I mean, I'm a writer. It's part of the fun of writing. Real life isn't that compressed: people don't say things that well. But in writing you can put in a character and make it come out anyway you want. In the album it's a situation of people experiencing ecstasy or they want to have ecstasy or they have tasted it but they can't hang onto it. Or they're thinking about how to get it, where is it, what is it, what does it mean?" 2000

"We were searching around for an engineer and Mike had been talking about this guy Tim Laken. And it turned out that Tim lived only a few blocks from me, so we had Tim over. And I was playing him some stuff. And I said, 'This is one of my favourite, favourite things. This is the kind of thing I'm interested in', and I played him 'The Blue Mask'. This, here, this is what I want. I want better than this. This is a good place to start. He said, 'I love the guitars on that. I know I can give you that.' So I said, 'OK'. And did 'Like A Possum'. It started with my friend P Cornish who lives outside London, a true genius. He's a sound designer. He makes things. I've got a bunch of toys from him. Just before going into the studio, this box arrived. His note said, 'This is a present only to be used when you go into the studio'. And that's the sound that we have on 'Like A Possum'. So I took it out, just plugged it in and started playing it immediately. It was like, Oh my God. So I called Mike and said, You have got to get over here and listen to this thing. And I came up with the 'Possum' riff and then Mike and I played it over and over. We would just play it for hours. Hours of doing that just did something wonderful. So then it was

SOLO IN THE NOUGHTIES

just a matter of figuring out a way to sing it and the lyrics to put to it. We went through a lot of things before I got to where I was meant to be. In the end, it was in three sections. And when we played it back we didn't know it was eighteen minutes long. It didn't seem that long. I just though it was monumental. "'Possum' really had to do with focus and concept. The lyrics were written out, but they had to be adjusted. I mean, they worked. We went in and tried it out. The guys only played it once in the studio and that was it. I was going to play that a couple of times and take the best one, but we did this once and that was the end of it. The vocal then had to be adjusted to it, which is why it sounds improvised. It's gorgeous. It's amazing. It's really amazing loud. You may not believe this but we sat listening to it about five times in a row. And we just couldn't believe it! I remember going, We did it, we did it! Listen to that. It's awe inspiring. It's absolutely everything it's supposed to be. I just can't believe it. We put it on big speakers and just blasted it and just listened to it over. Forget about doing anything else. Here we are. Let's blast it. It's very big but it's not unfriendly. It's not trying to scare you or be dissonant or jar you. It's huge. I was telling everybody, It's big, it's sweeping, take your time. No big moves! Steady captain!" ON 'LIKE A POSSUM', 2000

"That's a piece with Jane Scarpantoni on cello and Fernando and Laurie (Anderson) on electric violin. It's a little piece of something. Of what? It's a secret. I don't want to tell you what that is. We had been listening to it and the variance of it for a while. I thought, I could put something else to this. It was like one minute long when it was done. It was like serendipity." ON 'ROUGE', 2000

"It's hard to believe it isn't. It's certainly set up so you could think that. These albums have continuance. My work should have a forward thrust to it as it winds its merry way. There's a universal chord to all of it. That's why *Hamlet* will forever be real. I mean, people can ponder over why Hamlet acts a certain way, forever, because there's a certain mystery to it. But there's things about it – his relationship to his father, his mother, Ophelia - that just hit you. You know that it's true, whatever it is, not that you can necessarily put it into words.**"**

ON WHETHER 'MODERN DANCE' IS A SEQUEL TO 'TRADE IN'
FROM SET THE TWILIGHT REELING, 2000

"I don't think of this album as dark at all, I see it as incredibly expansive.**"** 2000

"Friends like it just fine and some people are particularly impressed by the sound of the recording. It's like, How did you do that?" 2000

"We wanted a violin part on the tune and it was obvious who to ask. If you want unique, genius support, you have to call Laurie. She listened to the track and came up with an astonishing part that only she could come up with.**"** ON 'ROCK MINUET', 2000

"I thought with 'Baton Rouge' you could make it into a really great pop song. Big strings and drums and all that stuff. I had thought of doing that for a while. And we tried recording the song and it was the hardest song to record on the whole album. It was amazing how hard it was. You would think it's so simple. There are things in there that are strange rhythmically and jumps that take place. Wilner said, Just record it like you did at your home studio and forget about a record 'record' version. Just go out and sing it the way you did in the first place. So we went out and recorded it as a trio and that was the one that worked."

ON 'BATON ROUGE', 2000

SOLO IN THE NOUGHTIES

❝I've been thinking about recording this album for years. Everything we had we put in there. All my albums have been real attempts to get to that place, but this one really went there, down to the last dot. I wouldn't change a thing. I really love the songs.❞ 2000

❝I like those kind of things and I like what Hal does on that. Steve Bernstein was the guy who did the horns. I don't know if you noticed, but when it starts out the bass sound is huge. It was built around that, that bass sound. It was like, Oh my god, listen to that. I mean, Jesus. It's right in what we call the pocket. It was Fernando. That's a heavy overdriven bass. The way it happened was I got one of my pedals and was like, Fernando, do you have a minute? And he plugged in and it was like ROAARRR and he went RRRR when he heard the bass through my pedal. He had to get out of the room where the bass was. He was like, My god what an amazing sound! It was great fun. It was also about giving a letter to every little mental aberration. Psychosis in the key of C. Matricide – C. I was just having fun.❞

ON 'PARANOIA IN THE KEY OF E', 2000

The Raven (2003)

❝It's not spoken word. Not. Spoken. Word. Spoken word sounds like a biography of Winston Churchill read to you by Ian McKellan or something, okay? This is not spoken word. It is acting with sound effects with a cast of thousands. It's fun. Spoken word is like someone telling you about trigonometry. That's not what this is. People don't know how to refer to it. Some people say it's like an old radio play. We've got all these incredible effects.❞ 2003

❝Working with Willem Dafoe and Steve Buscemi is about as much fun as you can legally have. Having them act out your words is fantastic. They're professional actors and I was lucky to have them. They were really doing me a favor. They said they were fans of mine, thank God, so it worked out really great.❞ 2003

"I just wanted to have a good time. That's always been my motivation. I've always thought of rock as a very freeing thing. I feel really great when I'm doing it and listening to it, dancing to it, playing it. I really like that. I wanna have fun, that's it. I don't wanna work. And I've gotten away with it so far." **2003**

"It's what the world identifies with. It's compulsive, obsessive, anxious — paranoia. This essay he wrote, *The Imp Of The Perverse,* now I took that title and wrote a little play called 'Imp Of The Perverse' in the album. I was just writing in the style of Poe, because Bob Wilson had said to me, 'Can you write a little Freudian take on Poe?' And that's what it was. For better or for worse. Anyway, what was the question? What pulls you toward Poe's work? The theme: Why am I so attracted to that which I know is bad for me?" 2003

SOLO IN THE NOUGHTIES

" Poe has this essay called *The Imp Of The Perverse*. It's about why are we attracted to things we know are bad for us. That's as universal a trait as exists. I don't know anyone that can't relate to that one. People who smoke, people who are overweight, people who drink, every 12-step program in the world. Everybody in everyday life knows about that and that's what Poe is writing about. He's the father of obsessive-compulsive behaviour in writing. He goes straight through the work of my favourite authors, William S. Burroughs and Hubert Selby Jr. This is a guy who wrote *Murders In The Rue Morgue*, the first detective story. Can you imagine doing that? My God! He predicted the big bang theory in this long poem he wrote about the universe called 'Eureka'. Whoa! Imagine doing all that. "

2003

" **The intense detail of the work, whether it be composition or recording or mixing, could be maddening at times but it's satisfying to feel a sense of completion. I can finally let out an exhaling breath and feel like I've done myself, this project and Poe proud.** " 2003

“There's something about ambiguity that drives people crazy. They want confirmation of whatever they suspect. They want tidy definitions. They want a black and white world when shades of grey can be far more interesting. The problem is that once something or someone is so clearly defined, there are occasionally limitations and boundaries placed around a person and his or her work. In terms of me and this project, I found Poe's work far more interesting and worthwhile of exploration. I'll leave the speculation to others.” **2003**

“It required total immersion into his work and into his language, which I've always had a great affection for. To me, his use of words slips right into my idea of what rock and roll can be: rhythm and intensity and pure power.” 2003

Animal Serenade (2004)

“To me *Animal Serenade* is not just another Lou Reed live album. It's a studio album with an audience.” **2004**

SOLO IN THE NOUGHTIES

WITH MOBY, IN NEW YORK, AUGUST 2004

Lou On Other Music

“Frank Zappa's probably the single most untalented person I've heard in my life. He's a two-bit pretentious academic, and he can't play rock'n'roll, because he's a loser. And that's why he dresses up funny. He's not happy with himself and I think he's right.” 1967

“David tried to help the cat - Iggy. David's brilliant and Iggy is stupid. Very sweet but very stupid. If he'd listened to David or me, if he'd asked questions every once in a while, I'd say, 'Man just make a one-five change and I'll put it together for you. You can take all the credit.' It's so simple, but the way you're doin' it now you're just making a fool out of yourself. And it's just gonna' get worse and worse. He's not even a good imitation of a bad Jim Morrison and he was never any good anyway.” **1975**

“We had vast objections to the whole San Francisco scene. It's just tedious, a lie and untalented. They can't play and they certainly can't write. You know, people like Jefferson Airplane, Grateful Dead are just the most untalented bores that ever came up. Just look at them physically, I mean, can you take Grace Slick seriously? It's a joke! It's a joke! The kids are being hyped.” 1967

"Gangster rap is boring to me but that's because I've been out in the streets a long time." **2003**

"I was aware of Jonathan Richman at all times. He's like my little brother." 2003

"Ornette Coleman's been an idol of mine ever since I heard him in the Sixties." **2003**

"I could take Hendrix. Hendrix was one of the great guitar players but I was better." 1975

"I have been in awe and in love with Ornette Coleman and Don Cherry since the first note I heard from them. It's influenced every cell in my body, but I'll never play like them. But that idea is in me." **2004**

LOU ON OTHER MUSIC

WITH DAVID BOWIE AND IGGY POP, 1973

LOU REED *Talking*

❝I heard your album *Is This It?*. We were listening to it in the studio. It was great. All those great guitar parts. You know, it's very difficult to play like that. It sounds simple, but it's not easy to do. I thought it was great that bands are making music like that again.**❞** LOU REED TO THE STROKES, 2004

THE STROKES

❝Lou's been a really great friend to me and a great advocate of my work. I find it a little overwhelming to be honest because he really has done so much for me. It's kind of blown my mind. He's been sort of a mentor, talks me through stuff all the time. I've learned so much from him as an artist, you know, just being around his intuitive approach to playing; it's a privilege.**❞**

ANTONY OF ANTONY & THE JOHNSONS, 2005

The Tao Of Lou

❝I try very much, whenever I do projects, whatever it is, there's only one thing on my mind, only one thing. And nothing interferes with that, it doesn't matter, the house could be burning down, really.❞ 2003

❝You know the expression 'God protects fools and drunks'? I qualify for both.❞ **2000**

❝I look forward to it every single night, no matter how small the city is.❞ 2003

❝I think rock is folk music. I think the electric guitar is just an extension of the wandering minstrel – you know, in those old days in England when they're traipsing around and putting on plays and singing, that's a rock band today.❞ **1995**

❝It's depressing when you're still around and your albums are out of print.❞ 2000

❝One of the nice things about getting older is getting to know yourself and what exactly you really are or it could be one of the not nice things about getting older, too, I suppose. It takes time to find that out what you really mean, what you really do, what you really respond to. Some people may not like what they find, and some people just try to get better with what they've got. You're dealt a certain hand - how are you going to play it?❞ 2003

LOU REED *Talking*

❝If there's something I can't figure out, before I go to sleep, I'll be thinking about that and assuming I can still sleep because I'm thinking about that, when I wake up, it'll be figured out.❞ **2000**

❝**So many things happened to me out of the blue, fell in my lap. I was doing zero, absolutely zero. I find sometimes that zero is the way to get things happening. That's a very Zen kind of attitude. Sometimes you have to be able to read the lay of the land when it's time to claw and fight and bite. And then other times it's time to take a hike.**❞ 2002

❝Well, that's what I find, that's called instinct. Even if it may take a little while to see the results. Something really flops into your lap like a giant bird with a golden egg.❞ **2002**

❝**Shovelling coal in a coal mine? That's work. Playing guitar? I don't call that work.**❞ 2005

"I was telling a friend of mine, Oscar, a novelist, that I was born on the outside and have stayed there. Probably one of the reasons I'm still around is because I've never made any attempt to be on the inside. I have less to do with these people and I can't fulfill their expectations. Anyway, they don't like what I do, and I don't like them either actually. I walk away because I can only take so much of music industry nonsense before it starts to get debilitating or depressing: the people you deal with, the judgments they're making, what they want, what they expect, how they hope to sell, who they're aiming at, how low the bar gets to be. But at a certain point, I think people learn not to come to you for certain projects. You're just the wrong person. They know that it's hopeless."

2002

"Me, I've concentrated on music pretty much to the exclusion of other things. And even within that to sound and tone. And I'm good for hours on that particular subject. Magnets and speakers, gears, tubes, what kind of tubes, wood, what makes a good guitar. All my stuff's custom. That's what I do. I mean, there are peripheral things I do, I do photography, I write plays, I have books published, but that's neither here not there. Essentially it's been concentrating on this one thing. I'm not joking around when I've said occasionally, trying to learn how to play a D chord properly has been a very big thing for me. The exact way to get this tone, which I can now do all the time, has taken forever, it seems like forever. When I think about that for X number of years experimenting with wood and pickups, if you actually thought about it you'd say, that person's crazy. But that's what I do." 2003

THE TAO OF LOU "

❝People here argue about which is more disgusting - the movie business or the music business. Just depends which way you would rather be raped and pillaged.❞ **2003**

❝**I remember the first time I read, *Fear And Loathing In Las Vegas*. I know the opening of the book by heart. It was one of the funniest things I have ever read. When authorities destroy what is true and rightful, it is always important to work against them. Hunter S. Thompson did that. He was one of the funniest writers who ever lived. It is horrible to think that we'll never get anything new from him. He is a classic. He told the truth. I was really sorry when I heard he was dead. I was going to do a reading with him in New York a while ago. He had used one of my lyrics in something he had written. But then he got stuck in traffic and the whole thing came to nothing. Everything he wrote was good. And funny. He was speaking out against everything that was stupid. Against very sick powerful people. He was a real star.❞** 2005

❝I have a very short attention span, and have to always compensate for it.❞ **2003**

❝**I studied Mr Warhol. Any dot that I can use from him, I do. How many times do you get to be around geniuses? What I call geniuses. I think he qualifies.❞** 2005

❝You practice long enough, you get better. You just get better. Some of the things that were very hard for me to do musically then, I can do much better now and far more easily. And more confidence about things makes certain writing possible. There are degrees of compassion and detail that I'm aware of now that I know I wasn't then. I think the depth of the lyrics is more sophisticated than it was. I have a lot more experience to pull on, to make stories. Can I do twelve really, really fast songs in a row and not collapse in a heap? Probably not. But I can do a couple of uptempo really heavy ones and I can do

some mid-tempo killer things and it can go on for a while, with a depth that's really incredible. I couldn't have done that in my twenties, I know that.**"** **1995**

"What I really want more than anything else is to quit smoking. That's what I want. I've quit a lot of things in my life, and this one's the worst. Maybe 'cause it's the last." 2000

"I often ask myself, 'What would Andy do? His philosophy was work, work, work, 24 hours a day. He could never understand why I didn't write fifteen songs a day.**"** **2004**

"I can't do anything I want to. I mean, I can't have my own TV show. I can't have my own movie. But within my little world, nobody tells me what to put on the albums." 2000

"I always hear music in my head.**"** **2000**

"You may be drawing a circle for the thousandth time, but maybe it's a slightly better circle." 2000

"You're a musician: You play. That's what you do.**"** **2000**